On the Threshold of History

Roy Burrell

Oxford University Press 1988

Oxford University Press, Walton Street, Oxford OX2 6DP

Oxford New York Toronto
Delhi Bombay Calcutta Madras Karachi
Petaling Jaya Singapore Hong Kong Tokyo
Nairobi Dar es Salaam Cape Town
Melbourne Auckland

and associated companies in
Beirut Berlin Ibadan Nicosia

Oxford is a trade mark of Oxford University Press

© Roy Burrell 1988
ISBN 0 19 917100 9

Typeset by MS Filmsetting Limited, Frome, Somerset

Printed in Hong Kong

Acknowledgements

The publishers would like to thank the following for permission to reproduce copyright material:

Aerofilms 6 btm, 120 (both), 121, 123 right, 127 btm;
Ardea 16 top left, btm left, 23 btm;
British Museum 16 btm right, 17 btm left, centre right, 31 top right, 40, 41 top, 54 btm, 55, 71 top, 88 btm left and right, 90 btm, 100, 101, 102;
British Museum (Natural History) 7 (all three), 8, 17 btm right;
C M Dixon 119 left, 126 left;
Egyptian Department of Antiquities 85;
Werner Forman 79, 98 top;
Robert Harding 14, 51 (both), 71 btm, 91 top, 93 top left, centre, top right btm left;
Hirmer Photoarchiv 61 right, 62 left, 71 centre, 106;
Michael Holford 16 top right, 17 top left, top right, 41 btm, 42, 59 (both) 68, 76, 82 btm, 83, 88 top left, 104, 105 left, 115, 117;
Chris Honeywell 86 left;
Illustrated London News 43, 86 right, 92 (both);
Institute of Archaeology 23 top;
Metropolitan Museum of Art, New York, 94, 95 top and btm;
Musée de l'homme, Paris 27 top left;
National Museum of Antiquities of Scotland 119 right;
Ronald Sheridan 30 (both), 31 left and btm right, 33, 54 top, 61 left 62 right, 66, 82 top left, top right, 91 btm, 93 btm right, 105 right, 122 top, centre left, centre right, and btm;
John Topham Picture Library 6 top, 57 top left, top right, 127 top right;
Wales Tourist Board 37;
Rogert Wood 98 btm.

Illustrations are by Steve Ashley, Chapman and Bounford, Peter Connolly, John Fraser, Peter Kesteven, Chris Molan, Tony Morris, David Salariya, Graham Smith, Tony Smith, Techniques, Michael Whittlesea and Maurice Wilson.

Contents

The first man-like creatures

When you last read about historical characters such as Julius Caesar, Francis Drake or Napoleon, did you ever stop to think that your ancestors were alive at the same time? 'Well, of course,' you might say, 'or I shouldn't be here now.'

Yes, but let's take it back a little farther. Your great, great (how many 'greats'?) grandfather must have been alive when the pyramids were being built in Egypt. Earlier still, members of your family hunted mammoths in the old stone age.

How far back have we to go to find our earliest relations? The deeper we peer into the past the less evidence there is. All we have from a period just over two million years ago, are a few stones and bones – hardly enough to fill a shoebox – so we'll have to use our imagination to picture these first human beings.

Suppose we are standing on the shore of a lake in East Africa. We can't see very much, for it is scarcely dawn. Before long the swirls of mist will be burnt away by the sun's rays and it will be very hot.

The shore is sandy with scrubby bushes. Nearby, a stream comes down from the hills and on its banks there are fig trees and acacias with sharp thorns. Away from the lakeside the forest is thicker and alive with game – wild pigs, monkeys, baboons and many different types of antelope.

Then suddenly we catch sight of a group of creatures who have spent the night at the water's edge. There are about twenty of them. They are a tribe of 'near' men – almost human but still partly animal.

There are two elderly males sitting together and making noises at each other. Are they talking? Some of the younger males are searching for stones to use as weapons. The females are sharing out the fruit, roots and nuts they collected yesterday. Later on, they will forage about near the camp site for fresh supplies.

Then the children appear – tiny things playing a chasing game round the bushes. None of the creatures is wearing clothes and all (except the youngest) are very hairy. The tallest adult scarcely tops five feet.

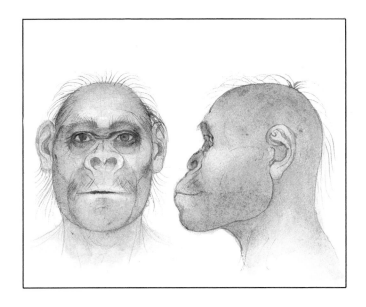

Their faces are somewhat strange. Their mouths are farther forward than their noses which are small and rather flat and they have no chins to speak of.

One of the young males is standing waist deep in the water, a stone poised in his hand. His keen eyes have seen a fish in the shallows of the lake but before he can strike, a shout from the bank distracts him. One of the tribe is pointing past him to what looks like a rotten log. It is a crocodile and there is a flurry of foam as the stone thrower scrambles to safety. Farther out, some hippos are making their grunting laughs and blowing as they float on the lake's surface.

After they have eaten, four or five of the young males go out hunting. They don't often kill game themselves, although they try to hit animals with the stones they have picked up. Usually they find their meat dead or dying. Today they are lucky. Only an hour's march from camp they come across a young impala caught in a thorn bush. It has died of starvation and other meat-eating predators have not been able to get at it.

The men cast about for stones and the tallest of them strikes a large pebble against another. Soon he has several jagged-edge cutters. Using them as saws they cut through the thorn branches until they can drag out the dead antelope.

They take it in turns to carry the carcase back to camp. They also take the sharp stones with them to cut up the meat.

Those left behind greet their arrival with shouts of joy. Meat is not an everyday treat, so they are delighted. They all cluster round while the impala is skinned and cut up.

One of the children reaches for a piece and his hand is angrily slapped away by an adult. No cooking is done: the tribes people don't know about fire and their meal is eaten raw.

An old woman sitting on a rock pauses with her food half way to her mouth. She lifts her head and looks in our direction. Her nostrils flare and her ears move slightly. We had better go before we alarm them.

The world's changing shape and climate – ice ages

This house is hanging over a cliff. Your first thought might be, 'Why build so close to the edge?' The answer, of course, is that it wasn't close to the cliff when it was put up – the sea has smashed a lot of the coast away.

This picture shows Rye in Sussex – a port during the Middle Ages but now some three miles from the sea.

The shape of Britain must have changed since we began to keep records of our history – say, over the last thousand years or so – but not so much that you couldn't recognise a map drawn in 1400, for example.

However, a thousand years is not a long period of time in the four and a half billion years of the earth's history, and the sea is not the only force of nature to alter the map of the world. There have been earthquakes, volcanoes, meteorites, floods, snow and ice.

It's easy to understand how, millions of years ago, giant upheavals of the earth's crust thrust sea beds high and dry in the air. How else could we explain the fossils of sea creatures 20,000 feet up in the Himalayas?

What about snow? If you've ever been in a snow-fight, you'll know that if you squeeze a snowball, it turns to ice. The same thing happens with ordinary falls of snow, provided the weather stays cold.

Normally it snows in the winter and then, when the temperature rises in the spring, the snow turns to water and runs away into ditches, streams, rivers and, finally, the sea. But if it never got warm enough to melt the snow, there would still be a white carpet lying on the ground when the next winter's snow came down.

For reasons which no one really understands, the whole world's weather got much colder than it is today about one and a half million years ago. The years went by and snow fell on snow for centuries. The bottom layers of flakes turned to ice because they were squeezed by the weight lying on them.

In mountainous places the masses of snow slid down the hill-sides and valleys to form slow-moving rivers of ice, or glaciers, as we call them. The glaciers joined up and spread out over the lowlands, particularly in the northern part of the world. At one time, most of Britain was covered with ice sheets hundreds or thousands of feet thick.

Glacier spreading down to the lowlands

As these sheets moved they acted like bulldozers on the rocks below them scraping and tearing away granite and limestone and pushing ridges of pebbles and boulders in front of them.

Smoothing plains flat and scouring out rocky valleys were not the most important results of the ice ages. Because there was so much water locked up in ice and snow, sea levels dropped all over the world – perhaps as much as 350 feet. The outcome of all this was that there was no North Sea and no Irish or English Channels. Our modern east coast rivers, the Trent, Humber, Tyne and Thames ran on to become tributaries of the River Rhine which didn't reach the sea until it was just south of the bottom of Norway.

Such ice ages went on until about 10,000 years ago – we think there may have been six or seven of them. In between the cold spells were periods of warmer climate, some of them tropically hot. Fossil remains of lions and hippopotamuses have been found in the Thames valley.

So much of the northern world was uninhabitable that Man could develop only in the warmer regions. Progress was painfully slow and the knowledge that Man picked up spread equally slowly.

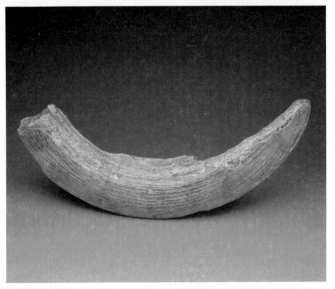

Fossils from the Thames Valley: bison horn, elephant tooth, hippo tooth

7

Neanderthal man

One type of early Man was called 'Homo Erectus'. This means 'Upright Man' but the name is not a very good one because we are fairly sure that man-like creatures had been walking on their hind limbs for thousands of years before his appearance.

However, he had a more complete kit of stone tools than his ancestors, including the examples shown below.

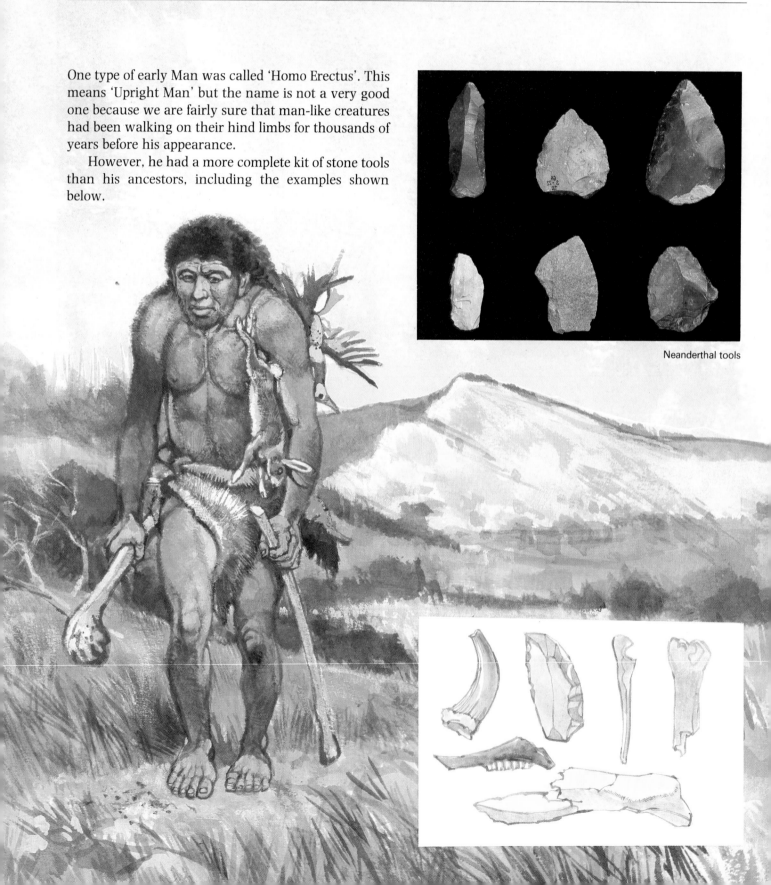

Neanderthal tools

It is quite likely that he knew how to use fire. He could move from one country, or even one continent, to another over the land bridges which had formed when sea levels dropped. These journeys from Africa to the rest of the world probably began about one and a half million years ago. Upright Man doesn't seem to have stayed in Europe when the ice ages started but later members of his family came back.

Some of these descendants are known as Neanderthal Men from the place where their remains were first found. Neanderthal Man was the first human being to live in Europe during the cold spells – partly because of his ability to make both clothing of animals skins, and fire.

For a long time it was thought that he had been a sort of 'sub-human' creature. His bony remains suggested that he looked more like some species of ape: that he shuffled along with dangling arms and slightly bent legs. His skull had large bony 'eyebrows' and a backward sloping chin.

However, it is now known that the size of his skull was as large as, or even larger, than some modern ones. Neanderthal Man was no fool. He had a good array of tools made of wood and stone.

He is the first human being known to have had some artistic and religious thoughts and ideas. He seems to have believed in some sort of after life. The skeleton of a boy was found in Russia. The body had been carefully buried and was surrounded by ibex horns arranged in a circle.

On the other hand, some of the Neanderthal remains found point umistakably to the fact that parts of them had been eaten – by other Neanderthals? Of course, several types of Early (and even Modern) Man also thought that eating people was all right, so Neanderthal Man was not some strange exception.

From an examination of the remains, it seems that these creatures were fairly healthy although the bones were sometimes slightly arthritic. Their teeth show hardly any signs of decay, even in the most aged. An adult could expect to live about thirty years although a few managed to survive to forty or fifty.

The really strange thing about Neanderthals is not only where they came from but more remarkably, where they went. The first traces of this type of human being appeared about 150,000 years ago and they became common between eighty and fifty thousand years ago. No one is sure who their immediate ancestors were.

As we've seen, they turned up in many parts of the world and were probably the only type of human being to inhabit Europe during the early stages of the cold spells. A little later, Modern Man began to live in Europe also. Towards the end of the last ice age, Modern Man was left alone – Neanderthal Man had disappeared – not only from Europe but throughout the world.

Some Neanderthal sites

Modern man

This a picture of what scientists call 'Modern Man'. His ancestors appeared in Europe perhaps a quarter of a million years ago. His other scientific name is 'Homo Sapiens' which is Latin for 'Man of Wisdom'.

The type only became common about forty or fifty thousand years ago but when he did, his older cousins, the Neanderthals, seem to have died out completely.

If he were to walk down your road, dressed in jeans, sandals and a tee shirt, you wouldn't even bother to turn your head to look at him. He wouldn't appear any different from any other similarly dressed person you know.

For the time being, the series of changes in the bodies of his forebears had come to an end. Homo Sapiens was, in all important ways, exactly the same kind of creature as ourselves. From then onward his development would depend not upon him becoming taller, heavier, brainier or stronger but on his increasing ability to pass on his knowledge and skills and to alter the world about him and to shape it into what he wanted.

He already knew how to make and use fire, how to chip flint into tools and weapons and how to turn animal skins into clothes. In Europe these skills enabled him to live on the fringes of the icefields, getting his food by hunting and gathering.

Scene of everyday life soon after the ice age had ended

Old-fashioned ideas about our family tree

The scene is a fair on the frozen River Thames in the late 1600s. There are tents and stalls selling pies and ale; dice and card players are making a living from gullible visitors. There are acrobats, tumblers and tight-rope walkers. One man has a dancing bear and on the thickest part of the ice an ox is being roasted over a huge fire.

A crowd collects to watch an enormous man take on all comers at wrestling. Nearby is a tent, outside which a youth is shouting, 'Come and see the giant's skeleton! Walk up! Walk up! Only a penny to view the bones of a mighty ogre!' A line of people pay him and move slowly inside.

Once there, they gaze open mouthed at what is on display. An older man points out the items of interest. 'There were giants in those days, as the Good Book tells us,' he says. 'Look at these teeth.' He holds one up. It weights a couple of pounds. At the rear of the tent is a curtain. With a dramatic gesture, the man twitches it aside. A gasp goes up from the crowd. On the platform is a mighty backbone with a forest of ribs extending from it. To emphasis the proportions, a young boy stands inside the rib cage.

The spectators gape for a while and then make their way out, muttering to each other about this wonder of the world – the mortal remains of a giant who must have been, in life, about twenty feet tall.

Of course, if a modern expert could have been present, he would have recognised the exhibit for what it was – not a giant but the headless and limbless remains of a mammoth.

Very few Europeans in those days had even seen an elephant, let alone a mammoth, so it isn't surprising that they should have been fooled. It took many years of patient work by scientists before the general public had any notion of extinct animals, the great age of mankind and the vast history of the world itself.

A modern scientist finds out as many facts as he can and then builds a theory to account for them. Later on, when fresh information comes to hand, the theory may have to be changed, added to or scrapped altogether. But before the scientific method was established, facts were thin on the ground and often ignored if they contradicted a pet theory.

Some of the old-fashioned ideas seem very far fetched to modern ears. For instance, James Ussher in the 17th century declared that, from his calculations, the world was created in the year 4004 B.C. A Dr. John Lightfoot agreed with him and added that this important event had happened on 23rd of October at nine o'clock in the morning!

Regarding the early history of Britain, there were plenty of suggestions as to who the first settlers might have been. Egyptians, Greeks, Romans, Trojans and Phoenicians were all put forward at one time or another. Even the sons of Noah or the lost tribes of Israel were named as the ancestors of the Britons. From the 1600s onward, the Druids were held responsible for almost every ancient and unexplained landmark that was not obviously natural!

Most people did not worry themselves overmuch about such matters: they were too busy earning a living to spend time in idle guessing games. Their attitude seemed to be that searching for our past was a sheer waste of time. It was unknown and unknowable. If someone wondered about the origin of the layers of rock plainly visible in cliffs and quarries, he would be told that they were the remains of the Great Flood mentioned in the Bible. What appear to us as unmistakable tools of flint were dismissed as elfshot, thunderbolts, bits of shooting stars or even fairy arrows.

In the 19th century, the recently discovered cave art of the stone age was ignored or put down to the doodlings of tramps or idle soldiers. However, the evidence was beginning to pile up that man had lived on the earth for a very long time indeed. The thousands of millions of years the earth had been in existence was a timespan far beyond the imagination of anybody.

How we know

These archaeologists are at work, digging up the things that will tell us about our past. Let's ask one of them what he does to date the objects.

'Well,' he says, 'before we do that, it might be a good idea to mention the work of Hutton, Lyell and Darwin. One of the men who questioned the notion that a single flood had shaped the entire earth was James Hutton, a Scottish geologist who lived in the 18th century. He believed that some rocks were laid down under water as layers of mud or sand pressed hard by new layers on top. He thought that the process must have been a very slow one.

'Another Scot, Sir Charles Lyell, showed that geological changes are still going on. He noticed for instance, that waterfalls continue to wear the rock over which they pour. If the rate of wearing and the amount of rock worn away could be worked out, it ought to be possible to say how long the waterfall had been running. For Niagara Falls, a period of millions of years seemed to be the answer.

'This fitted in very well with the theories of Charles Darwin. Darwin said that all living creatures have been slowly changing form over the centuries and that, to reach their modern shape, a very, very long time must have gone by – not just thousands of years but thousands of centuries.

'Now let's get back to your question. Of course, we have much better methods of measuring the age of rocks than any of the men I've mentioned – and we can be pretty sure of some plant and animal remains too.

'It's easy enough to see that the lowest layer of mud, dust or sand must be the oldest – provided that the layers haven't been overturned by an earthquake. Supposing you can identify the oldest layer, then anything in it must be older than anything in the layers above it.'

'Can you say how much older?'

'Not just like that, no. You can see why not if I say that a certain village pond has been there for a thousand years and there is a foot of mud at the bottom, it should follow that a layer or 'stratum' of similar material eighty feet thick is 80,000 years old.

'Unfortunately, it doesn't follow! The thickness of the stratum depends on a number of unknowns – the depth of water, the amount of silt in it, the average temperature and many other things.

'Fortunately, this century has seen some new ways of measuring, even if roughly, the actual age of samples of rock, wood, bone and other materials.

Diagram showing the different layers under the earth

'All these things are made of different kinds of chemicals and scientists know that some substances rot away much more slowly than others. When I say 'slowly' I really mean it – the time taken for the rotting or decaying may be thousands or even millions of years. Each chemical has its own time scale. We can use a machine to measure how much of the chemical has gone – a third, a half, three quarters or whatever it might be. From this we can work out how old it is. It's a reliable way of dating something that we've found, provided that we remember it's only a rough answer. Of course if we aren't looking for actual dates we can drill plugs out of the seabed and find out what the climate was like thousands of years in the past. We can tell from the layers of dust, mud and sand brought up what kinds of summer weather there were say 20,000 years ago.'

'Aren't there any exact ways of dating what you find?'

'Not absolutely, although if you are lucky, there is a method which comes fairly close. You have to count tree rings.'

'Tree rings?'

'Yes. Trees grow by adding a shell of wood just under the bark each year – a wide ring (W) if conditions are good, a narrow one (N) if they aren't. This gives a special pattern, for example W,W,N,N,N,W,N,W, W,W,N, and so on. In a stump left from a recent tree felling, you can tell when its life began by simply counting the rings. You can also compare the pattern with an older tree, gradually extending the period backwards. In fact, you are only limited by the samples of timber you can find. If you are lucky, you might find a series of ring patterns going back several thousand years. Then you can take a piece of wood from where you are digging, match it on the pattern and say exactly how old it is – but it doesn't happen very often.'

'So you can tell – roughly at any rate – the age of rocks, and the remains of human beings, animals and plants?'

'Yes. All these methods have only come into use in the last few years. Some give only very rough and ready pointers to the age of a sample. Perhaps a more accurate way of doing it will be found – who knows?'

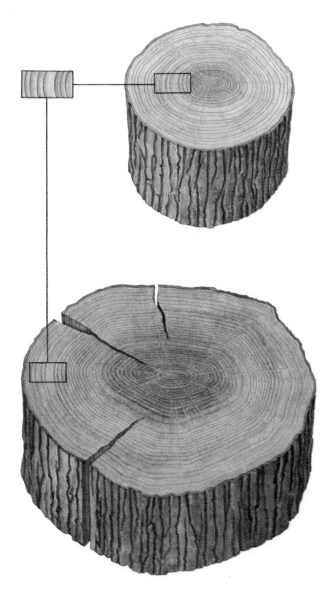

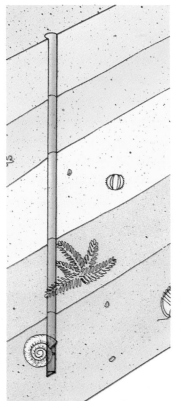

Sea bed drilling and bore

Comparison of young and old trees, showing the same ring pattern

15

Sticks and stones

Perhaps our archaeologist can tell us something about the tools and weapons used by early Man.

'Yes', he says, 'the manufacture of axes, knives, scrapers and other tools is perhaps the thing that really separates us from the animals. There have been many attempts to say exactly what the difference is between human beings and animals. Nearly all of these attempts fail. Whatever Man can do, some animals can also do, although perhaps only in a limited way.

'Human beings walk on their back legs, but so, for instance, do apes and bears – for a short distance at least. Man has speech, it has been said, and can exchange thoughts. But, to take only one example, our pets leave us in no doubt about their thoughts when they bark, mew, hiss, growl or purr.

'One suggested difference is, as I've already said, Man's use of tools and weapons. Again, some animals, particularly apes, will make and use simple implements. However, it seems that it is Man alone who makes tools and weapons for some future use, so perhaps this is the greatest difference.

'Several million years ago, early man-like creatures started to alter the shape of stones to make them handier implements. A man would take a fist-sized pebble and bang pieces off one end with another stone. Examples of these have been found in Olduvai Gorge in Africa and elsewhere.

'As the years went by men found out how to chip off pieces of stone all round the pebble, winding up with a pear shaped hand axe. The next step was to remove little flakes of stone from the edges, thus making a rough edge into a smooth one. A piece of flint can be razor sharp.'

'How do you know that the stones aren't just the result of a natural accident? Couldn't a couple of pebbles crash together in the sea, a river in flood, or perhaps a landslide?'

'There are two main ways of telling. If the stone has obviously come from somewhere else – because it isn't like the local rocks – then there's a good chance that it's been brought in. Secondly, when a stone has been split deliberately, it shows unmistakable 'ripple marks',

Chimpanzee using stick

Bear on back legs

Olduvai chipped pebbles

Wooden spear from Clacton

quite unlike anything in a stone that's been broken by a sharp frost or a forest fire, say.

'Of course, there's more than one way of chipping a flint. You can hit one stone with another, you can use a piece of wood or bone as a sort of chisel and remove flakes of stone by pressing, or you can hit your 'chisel' against your flint with a hammer stone.

'One development is quite interesting. That was to take a suitable lump of flint, trim it into a rough cylinder and then strike flakes off the edges. The flakes could be used as knives, borers, scrapers, chisels, drills and so on. The last stages of the old stone age show the first arrow heads, both with tangs and without.

'Flint was the favourite material of early Man but other rocks were also used – greenstone, obsidian and many others. As well as rock, stone age Man also had spears of wood.'

'How do we know about wooden spears? Surely wood couldn't survive from all those thousands of years ago?'

'Not normally but we do have at least one example. It was found at Clacton. Man used a flint scraper to straighten a suitable branch and to sharpen the end.

We think he then hardened the business end over a fire. Mind you, we've only got the point of the spear but it's enough.

'We've also got shaped and worked bones that must have been spear throwers. You fit the butt end of your spear into the notch and hold both the spear and the thrower in your hand. When you hurl your spear, the bone thrower sends it farther and faster than an ordinary spear on its own.

'Towards the end of the Palaeolithic period, as we call the old stone age, stone working didn't really improve, but the people who lived then were good at making things from bones, teeth, horns and antlers. As well as spear throwers, there were also chisels, scoops, scrapers, saws, awls or borers, needles for sewing, drills and lots more.

'They made necklaces of antler beads and bracelets from mammoth tusks but I suppose the most important use for wood or bone was as a handle for a stone tool. It's much easier to use then. Just try sharpening a pencil with only the blade of a penknife and you'll see what I mean.'

Acheulian hand axes

Flint hand axes

Stone flake and core

A spearthrower

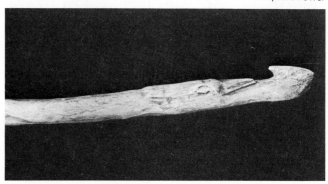

Cave mouth scene

Hunting

In the early days, it's quite likely that the only meat Man tasted came from creatures he found already dead – provided that he could scare off the hyenas and vultures. Throwing stones at them may have given him the idea of knocking down birds and small animals.

It must have needed considerable skill to hunt a particular creature rather than relying on luck. A good hunter learns to read the signs – a footprint, a broken leaf or blade of grass bent at an unusual angle. He has to find out all he can about the animal's habits, until he can almost get inside its mind. It's not much use looking for the prey in a place it rarely or never visits.

What does the animal eat? Where is its food found? Where does it drink and when? Because there are yearly changes in nature, the hunter will do better if he is able to read the coming and going of the seasons and to know when to expect these changes. A working knowledge of sun, moon and star movements would help him to be in the right place at the right time.

In order to hunt anything more than small game, he would have to co-operate with his fellow tribesmen. Man can't run as fast as a deer, not has he the sharp claws and fangs of a lion or tiger. But if he can make his quarry run away from him and towards his companion, his lack of speed doesn't matter. In addition, he can use sharp stones and wooden spears, even if his nails and teeth are not much use in killing.

He might follow a deer's trail for hours on end before getting within range, trying where possible to keep down wind of his target, so that his scent would not be carried to the animal and scare it off.

We don't really know but it seems likely that early human beings had keener senses than we do – or at least, they made better use of them. Some modern people, however, can narrow or widen their nostrils or alter the angle that their ears are set. These skills would be useful in picking up scent or sound signals. In the stone age perhaps everyone had these skills.

Two different ways of trapping animals

Mammoth hunter's camp

When it came to the hunting of really large animals, something more than sharpened senses was needed; there was always a better chance of success if several hunters could work together. Wild animals also sometimes hunt in packs – wild dogs, wolves and so on – but their success is more often due to weight of numbers rather than a well thought out plan.

For human hunters, language was essential, especially if there were last minute changes in the plan, which often entailed 'beating' or driving the chosen beast over a cliff or into a dead-fall trap. The latter is one where the animal is stunned by a rock or boulder which falls when the support is jerked away – probably triggered by a stumble into a rope stretched across the path. A pit trap is made by digging a large deep hole, covering it with branches and turf so that it looks quite natural. The prey is driven into it with shouts, spears and stones. Later on, when Man had learned to master it, fire was also used.

Towards the end of the last ice age, Man must have relied on his ability to hunt large game, as the climate was too cold to provide many of the seeds, fruit, and nuts that were commoner when the weather was warmer.

Among the biggest victims of the hunters were the cave bear, woolly rhinoceros and the mammoth. That the stone age hunters were successful is proved by the remains of their camps that have been found in several places in Europe – and, of course, by the fact that these huge, prehistoric elephants are now extinct.

Something that may account for their disappearance was Man's habit of picking the younger and more easily slaughtered mammoths. If modern elephants are anything to go by, it must have taken a female mammoth two years of pregnancy before her young one was born. At this slow rate of replacement, it wouldn't be long before the species died out.

Around the camps mentioned above, the remains of hundreds of these lumbering creatures have been found – ribs, tusks and spines. But mere bones are not our only evidence for the existence of the mammoth, as we shall see on the next page.

The Beretsovka mammoth

Perhaps we might have a word or two with a man who actually found a mammoth. He was a Russian peasant living at a place called Beretsovka in Siberia.

'No, it wasn't alive,' he says, 'In fact, the scientists told me it had been dead twenty or maybe thirty thousand years. I don't know about its age myself – just what was said at the time, back in 1908. I was interested, see, because I was the one that found it: well, my dogs did.

'Do you know much about this part of the world? No? Well, it gets very cold in the winter. Some say it's the coldest place on earth. I can't say about that but I do know that you'd burn yourself if you were fool enough to touch bare metal outdoors without your glove. In the spring, though, the rivers thaw and flow once more but the ground is only soft a few inches down. Below that it's frozen solid, summer and winter. They say it's been like that for thousands of years. They call it 'permafrost'.

'Well, I was walking home with my dogs along the river bank. It had been a hot summer and the permafrost started further down than usual. My attention was drawn to the dogs. They had run on ahead and were barking at what I took to be the top of a boulder sticking out of the marsh. When I got close I could see that they were tearing at it with their teeth. I called them off and went to have a look. I knew straight away that it was some sort of animal, so I told our village headman about it. He came to look and said we ought to report it to the authorities.

'It was only later that I started to kick myself. See, the skeletons of mammoths ('Mammoth' is a Russian word) are often turned up hereabouts and their tusks fetch a good price. We sell them abroad – to China, for example. However, it was too late for that. The scientists came down from St. Petersburg* late in the summer and dug it out.

'It was a mammoth all right. Complete with hair, hide, eyes, bones, meat and tusks. Those tusks are often more than ten feet long, so you can see why I was sorry I ever told anyone about it. Just think of all that ivory. Still I don't suppose I could have kept it a secret.

'Anyway, I suppose you know that the mammoth is, or was, a sort of elephant. Mammoths are extinct

*The old name for Leningrad which was the Russian capital then.

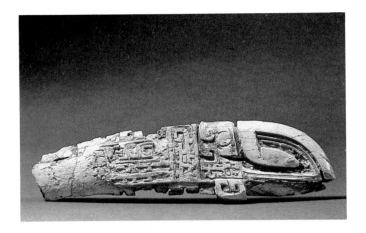

Carved mammoth ivory

'They said it looked a bit like the Indian elephant. That's to say not so big as the African one. It had a coat of curly hair that was a sort of orange brown colour with patches of thicker black bristles on its cheeks and sides.

'It was something to see, I tell you, but the scientists had even more marvels to tell us. They did a – what do you call it – a post mortem, that's it. Guess what! They could tell what it had eaten for its last meal all that time ago. Mostly grass of course but also poppies, thyme, sedges and all kinds of other wild plants. It didn't eat meat, see? Couldn't say the same about those eggheads from St. Petersburg. Would you believe it? They cut some meat from the carcase and grilled it. Said it tasted a bit gritty but I can't really say. They didn't give me any.

'The upshot was, they carted the skeleton and skin away – and those accursed tusks that should have been mine. They took them to the west and rebuilt a full-sized reconstruction in a museum. Perhaps it's still there. I don't really know.'

now. You know what that means? That's right, there are no more of them alive. They probably died out ten or twenty thousand years ago. My animal must have been one of the last of them.

'You should have seen it when they dug it out. All covered in mud it was. They said it must have wandered over the marsh when the ice sheet on top wasn't strong enough to hold its weight. The ice cracked, the mammoth went through and sank into the half frozen peat. Then the weather turned really bad and the poor old thing was sealed in solid.

Model of a mammoth

The origins of fire

Can you light a fire? If you are making one outdoors, you'll probably use newspapers and sticks of wood built into a cone around it. Strike a match and touch it to the paper. Provided that the wood is dry enough, the flames will catch.

How did primitive Man manage? He had no newspaper and no matches. In the beginning, he didn't manage at all. He ate his food raw and kept out of the colder parts of the world.

Of course, he was certainly aware of fire. He must have stared open-mouthed as a forest fire flared among the trees, caused perhaps by a bolt of lightning in a thunderstorm.

Maybe he overcame his natural fears and nervously stretched out an arm to pick up a smouldering branch. Waving it about with a little more confidence, he might have been surprised to see the flames rekindle at the far end. Could he have got the idea of a controlled fire at that moment? Dropping the branch on the ground could have set light to the dry grass.

This kind of thing probably happened over and over again through the centuries until the custom of having a fire was part of the tribe's everyday life. So Man could use fire but he still couldn't make it. When the tribe slept at night, there must have been some arrangement to make sure that the fire never went out. After all, you couldn't be certain of finding a forest fire whenever you wanted one.

We have no details but there must also have been some method of carrying fire when people were on the move: perhaps they had some material that would smoulder for days if need be and which could be blown into life when required.

We won't ever know how Man first hit on a way of making fire to order. He may have got the idea from rubbing his hands together. If you touch your own hands, palm to palm and rub them as fast and hard as you can, you'll stop before you've run out of energy or breath because your skin has become too hot to go on.

Could Man have reasoned that the same process with two pieces of wood might lead to a fire? We know that Man was using fire half a million years ago, but not whether it was made deliberately. Someone must have tried rasping one stick against another – probably without success until someone invented the drill.

Mastery of fire was a huge step forward. Fire had many uses – warmth and lighting are the most important but it could also be used for hardening spears, driving animals from their caves and for cooking.

Without some form of heating, Man could never have spread out to occupy the whole world and would have been confined to the tropical and semi-tropical regions where fires were not essential for survival.

Ways of making fire: 1 using a spindle,   2 using a bow drill,   3 using two stones to make a spark (providing one stone has metal in it),   4 rubbing a stick in a groove.

Food gathering and cooking

It's a common mistake to believe that early Man lived entirely on the meat from large animals. Kills of elephants must have been fairly rare throughout much of the old stone age. The meat of small creatures and from birds turned up far more often in the stone age diet. As well as these, there were many other items that could be collected by the tribe. Even in our modern world there is 'wild' food to be had. Many of us have eaten field mushrooms or hedgerow blackberries, for example, but early Man must have tasted far more types of berries than we do.

Nuts too provided a good deal of stone age food. Seeds from various plants were gathered in season. A great deal of tribal knowledge was necessary in order to be at the right place at the right time. It wasn't very much good if you weren't nearby when the seeds were ripe. By trial and error, people discovered which seeds were nice to eat, which not so nice and which made you ill or even poisoned you.

We can't be sure but it seems that the women and children did most of the gathering of roots, nuts, seeds and berries, whilst the men were more concerned with hunting. There were other forms of food to be had: from a rock painting, it can be seen that the honey of wild bees was always acceptable – even if it cost the honey stealer many stings!

Women digging up roots

Wall painting showing the collection of honey

to hold it near the glowing embers of the fire.

The first advantage of eating cooked food must have been that it tasted nicer but the second advantage is perhaps more interesting. It's a fact that most of the things you want to eat can be chewed up a lot quicker cooked than raw. Think how long an apple or potato would take to dispose of uncooked and compare the time taken if the food had been stewed or boiled.

The less time you take to eat, the more time you have for other interests, for example, making better tools and weapons. So perhaps it's not unfair to say that something as humble as cooking played a part in Man's upward climb towards civilisation.

Harpoons

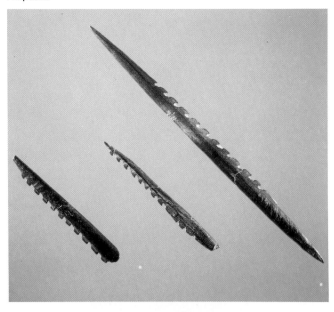

Another item on the menu, at least for some tribes, must have been fish. If you had the sea, rivers, lakes or ponds in your neighbourhood, it's almost certain you would have tried to catch some of the creatures that lived in them. We don't have any very early evidence for hook and line angling or even the use of nets so it seems that fish spears were the answer – or perhaps it's not so impossible to imagine that some peoples may have learnt how to poison a pond so that the fish would float to the surface – unconscious.

One of the biggest steps forward was the discovery of cooking. This was most likely the result of an accident – perhaps a portion of meat or fish fell into the fire, or was left on a stone too near it. However it happened, charred or grilled meat must have been the standard fare. There could have been no proper roasting before the invention of some kind of oven. There were no pots to hold liquids but it's just possible that some may have dug pits, lined them with clay, filled them with water which was brought to boiling point by having hot stones dropped in. In this way food could have been boiled but there is no evidence to say that anyone did so.

The most likely method of cooking was to spear a steak onto the sharpened end of a long, green stick and

Clothes

Animal skin used as protection

Although in very early times human beings were without clothes, the word 'naked' is probably not the right one to use. They were not far removed from animals and we don't usually think of a dog or a tortoise as being naked do we?

Why did we start to wear clothes in the first place? It's difficult to say but the answer may be a mixture of two or three reasons. These are often described as protection, warmth and modesty. Again, like cooking, the discovery of clothing was almost certainly an accidental one.

We'll never know how it came about but we can guess. Could it be that the uneatable skins of animals

that had been hunted were piled at the back of the rock shelter? Then maybe someone fell or rolled on them and found out how soft and warm the furs were. or it might be that those who chipped flints first spread a pelt over their laps to stop chips of stone cutting their skins. Again, someone could have wrapped a skin around himself before pushing through thorn bush country.

Whichever way the discovery was made, it is certainly true to say that without animal skins, Man would never have been able to move away from the warm parts of the earth to those areas where the weather was too cold for anyone to live without protection.

Let's ask one of the women what she has to do to make fur suits for her family.

'Well', she says, 'it depends what kinds of animal skins you've got to work with. If you have a lot of small animals, it takes a lot of sewing and that's not too easy. It's better to have a couple of large skins, if you can.

'Some hides have to be pegged out on the ground with pins of bone or wood. When they are stretched tight we take it in turns to scrape the inside of the skin. We use these specially shaped stones to do the work. Some skins have to be chewed to get them soft and pliable.

'We cut the shapes we need with flint knives, then we put two pieces together. We bore small holes along the edges with a sharp stone point.

'Using a chisel flint we can cut out a sliver from a suitable bone, shape and sharpen it and bore a tiny hole in the blunt end. Then a very thin strip of leather is threaded through the eye of the needle and we are ready to start sewing the pieces together.

'We only need complete suits of furs in really cold countries. They say that where our tribe came from, it was so warm that no one wore clothes at all. I just can't imagine a climate that hot.'

She goes on with her work and we move away. We wonder how long it will take them to discover how to make proper cloth from wool, cotton, linen or silk but it won't be in the old stone age. Hundreds of centuries will have to pass before any real progress is made. It's hard to imagine but consider the old stone age as a piece of string twenty or thirty feet long, and then guess what length of string you'd need for everything that's happened since – i.e. the middle and new stone ages, the copper, bronze and iron ages and the whole of recorded history right up to today?

Only a fraction of one inch for the whole lot!

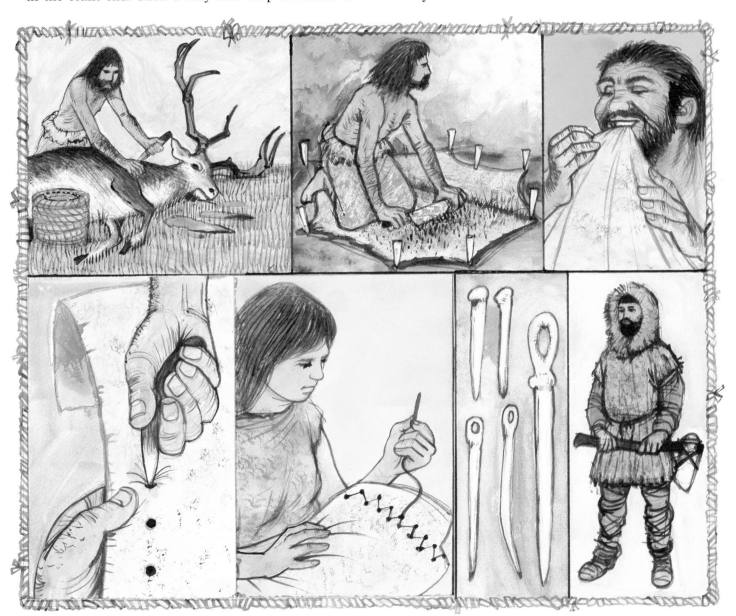

29

The artists

Painting of a bison from Altamira, Spain

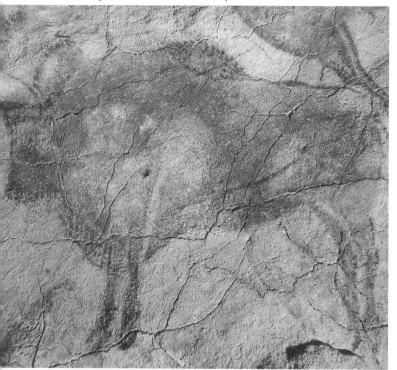

Painting of a horse from the caves at Lascaux, France

There is a widespread belief that all human beings of the old stone age spent all their time in caves. It's true that some people lived in caves, at least for some of the time. The belief arose because evidence for Man's existence is far more likely to survive in a cave than outside in the open air. Just before the middle of the last century, the first cave art was discovered.

In 1895 a man named Rivière found the first French cave with decorated walls. This was La Mouthe in the Dordogne and it came to light just twenty years after a Spaniard called Don Marcelino de Sautuola discovered the first Spanish cave paintings (of bison) on his estate at Altamira.

Probably the most famous 'painted' cave is the one at Lascaux, stumbled upon by French schoolboys in 1940. At this moment, we know of more than a hundred caves with 'picture galleries'.

At first, the historians of the time refused to believe that these beautifully coloured illustrations of wild animals could be the work of ignorant savages living in the old stone age.

Then it was pointed out that some of the animals shown were now extinct – either completely worldwide or at least locally. Furthermore there were places where the pictures were half covered by stone age rubbish or deposits of glassy stalactite. Quite often a cave is found whose entrance has been blocked for tens of thousands of years, yet still has walls covered with paintings.

At last the doubters were forced to accept that the animal pictures were indeed the work of 'savages'. Modern scientific methods have now managed, however roughly, to date the remains of fires used by the artists of Lascaux. It seems that the last flames must have flared some time between 15,500 and 17,000 years ago.

Certainly a fire or some form of lighting was needed by these ancient artists, since most of the art is a long way from the cave entrance. It is surely beyond the bounds of belief that anyone could have worked away in pitch darkness. In fact some primitive lamps have been found buried in cave floors. A typical specimen was a hollowed out lump of limestone for holding melted animal fat, whilst a twist of dried moss provided the wick. Animal fat may also have been used to mix the paints which were mainly different coloured earths – red, yellow or brown ochre plus chalk or carbon from the fire.

We don't know how the paint was put on – it could have been applied with a pad of fur or a brush made from a stick with a chewed end. The paint could have been rubbed on from a lump of coloured clay or even blown on as a powder through a hollow bone.

Sometimes an artist has left prints or stencils of his hands. He would coat his palm and fingers with colour and press it against the wall. For a stencil, he'd put his hand on the wall and paint round it. Apart from hands, an animal outline was often chiselled into the rock and the shape then filled in with colour.

Painting was not the only form of art left to us by stone age Man. He also made engravings with a sharp stone on bones, antlers and horns. Sometimes a statue in clay or limestone was tried.

In all the pictures we know of from Europe, the wild horse is the commonest subject but many other animals are represented – the woolly rhinoceros, mammoth, bison, aurochs (wild ox), red deer, elk, ibex, chamois, cave lion, cave bear, boar, hare and wolf. There are also drawings of salmon, trout, eels, dolphins and birds. Human beings are not very numerous but one thing you do find is an occasional 'composite' or imaginary animal. In addition, there are many mysterious signs or symbols, for example, lines, dots and oblong patterns.

We don't know why these pictures were made – perhaps there were many reasons, for instance: 1. decoration 2. a pastime 3. the tribe's special 'totem' animal 4. sympathetic magic – rather like a witch making a doll and sticking pins in it: in other words, the drawing of a deer with an arrow in it would make next day's hunting easier 5. drawing animals might make them more plentiful 6. teaching the youngest hunters what to look for and what to aim at 7. the recording of a particular hunt – important, perhaps, to a tribe without writing 8. maybe just a longing to leave something behind, rather on the lines of someone carving his initials, or even 'Kilroy was here'!

Whatever the reason, we have to remember that there are many examples of paintings one on top of the other, a fact which might affect our choice of the reasons set out above.

The record (so far) for these works of art must be held by the cave of Les Combarelles in France's Dordogne valley. Here there are over 200 representations of animals and more than a dozen of the mysterious signs.

Limestone lamp

Bone carving

Stencilled hand painting

31

Retreat of the ice sheets

No one can say for certain what caused the tremendous changes in the climate that have affected huge parts of the world, but we do know that during the last million and a half years, there have been something like six ice ages. In between them the weather became almost tropical, even in England. Hippos swam in the Thames

Northern Hemisphere showing the extent of the ice sheets

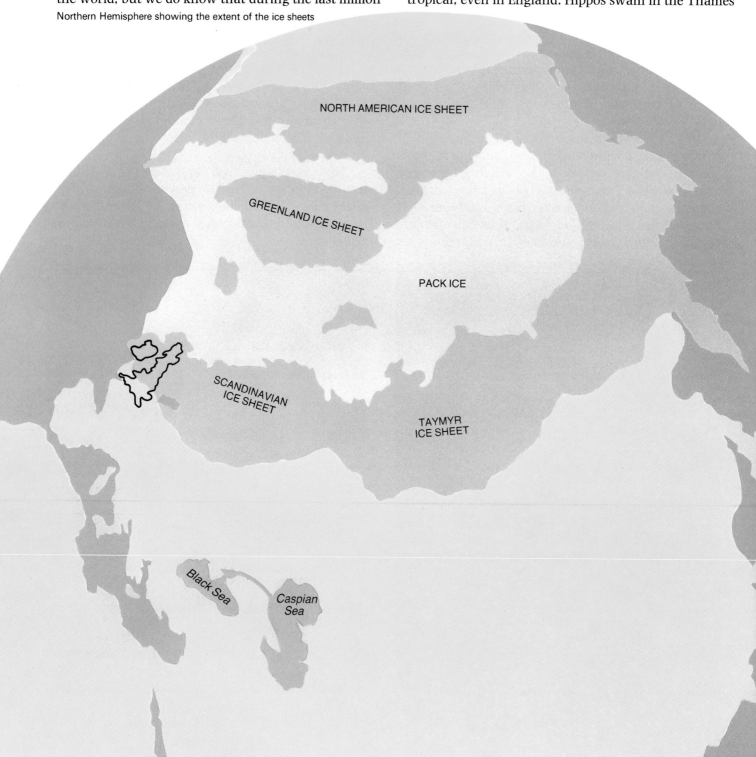

NORTH AMERICAN ICE SHEET

GREENLAND ICE SHEET

PACK ICE

SCANDINAVIAN ICE SHEET

TAYMYR ICE SHEET

Black Sea

Caspian Sea

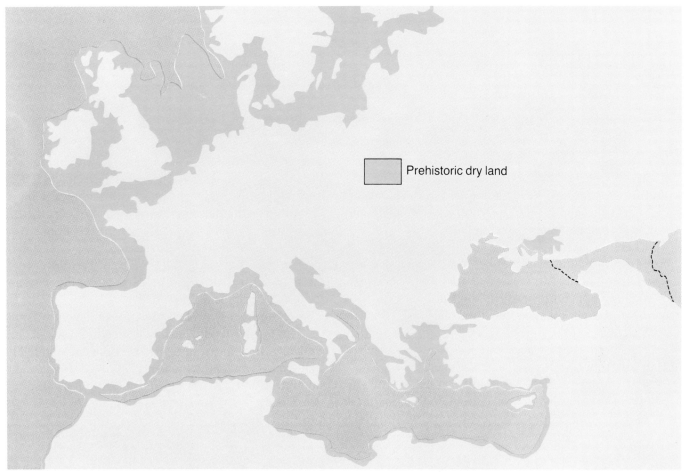

Prehistoric dry land

Ancient shoreline in prehistoric times

and lions stalked along its banks.

Roughly about 10,000 years ago (and we don't know the reason for this either), the average annual temperature started to rise little by little and vast stretches of the earth's northern regions began to be habitable once more.

Much of the ice melted and flooded low-lying areas, making islands of what had only been hills during the cold times. There were, naturally enough, many other changes. Rivers altered their courses, rain fell instead of snow. Man could live in areas that had once been too cold and he could do so with less clothing. The numbers and kinds of animals he hunted were different too. The cold-loving beasts, such as the woolly rhino, the mammoth and reindeer, unable to rid themselves of thick, furry coats, followed the retreating ice. A few species disappeared from some regions, others died out completely.

The human beings that still hunted for a living had to learn new ways. Fishing became more common and tools of bone and horn began to take the place of some types of flint implement.

Every time there was a warm period following an ice age there was an increase in the numbers of human beings. They slowly occupied more and more of the earth's surface and gradually increased their mastery of their surroundings.

This period between the last of the ice at the end of the old stone age and beginning of the new stone age is known as the Mesolithic, or middle stone age.

Reindeer antler pick

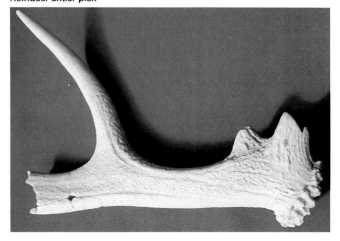

Hunting

In the middle stone age, Man still depended on hunting to provide most of the food for himself and his family. The animals his ancestors had hunted in the old stone age had gone and he had to learn all over again the habits of the beasts he wished to kill.

There were many ways of slaying his quarry – he could disguise himself in the skin of an animal in order to get near a herd of deer. The deer might have been red or roe deer but there were wild pigs and oxen, not to mention the elk eight or ten thousand years ago at places such as Star Carr in Yorkshire, or Abinger in Surrey. Both these places have yielded evidence of Man's presence in the middle stone age.

The hunter could lie in ambush, provided that he knew the animal's habits well enough to be sure that it would show up in a fairly short time. He could set a trap by putting a noose of cord in the right place. If it was across a path known to be used by whatever he was hunting, he might be lucky and have the beast thrust its head into the loop. As it struggled, the noose would tighten.

As at the end of the old stone age, the hunters could have used fire to drive game over a cliff or into a swamp, where it could be finished off.

Yet another way of taking an animal was by trailing it. The hunter would cast about for the track of, say a red deer. If he found one, his experience would tell him if it was worth following. It wasn't much good tracking along a spoor a week old – it had to be a reasonably fresh one.

Camouflage hunting with deerskins

If we could see such a tracker in action, what would he be doing? He would be looking at the signs the animal had left – a grass stalk bent or even broken and still oozing sap, a leafy twig torn from a tree, animal pellets or droppings, the beast's own scent or hairs rubbed off on bushes or tree trunks. And if the hunter's senses were too coarse to pick up this smell, he could use his new secret weapon – his dog.

The dog had most likely been taken as a puppy and trained to help with the hunt. He was the very first animal to be tamed by Man. If the quarry was not to be frightened, the hunter and his dog had to take care to keep down wind from it wherever possible, so that his scent would not be picked up by the target. Middle stone age Man probably used a couple of methods to tell the wind direction, particularly if the wind speed was very light. He could hold up a blade of grass or a dead leaf, let go and watch which way it fell. The other dodge was to lick a finger and hold it up. The side that cooled first showed the quarter from whence the wind was coming.

The actual killing of the prey would be done with sticks, stones, spears, or Man's latest invention, the bow and arrow.

There are lots of us today who, for various resons, dislike or condemn hunting and even refuse to eat meat at all. These opinions are to be respected but it is a fact that all our ancestors were hunters and meat eaters. If they had not been, we would not be here now.

Dugout canoes and coracles

Man may have taken to the water towards the end of the old stone age. However, it's only when we get to the middle stone age that we know that he used boats.

We think it probably started with people accidentally clutching branches or tree trunks when in danger of drowning. Perhaps they had slipped and fallen in or they might have tried to swim a river and found the current sweeping them out to sea.

However it happened, Man soon discovered that it's better to use a log to cross a lake or river rather than relying on his own skill and strength. For one thing it takes less energy and for another it's sometimes possible to stay drier by sitting astride the log and paddling with the hands.

He also discovered that a log could be prevented from rolling over and giving him a ducking by lashing a smaller log to a couple of its branches.

The next step was to improve his driving power. He could paddle with his hands, as we have seen, but he could get a better performance if the hands could be bigger and the arms longer. The only way to do this was artificially of course. The long arms and big hands were imitated by making oars or paddles from straight branches with flat plates of wood fastened to the ends.

The breakthrough came when Man found out how to make the first real boat shape. A log can be split with stone wedges to make a pair of dugout canoes. Let us look at one of the half logs, resting on its round side. On the flat top the boat builders dropped stones which had been heated in a fire. Before they cooled down, each stone had burnt a small patch. With sharp flints, the boat men scraped away the charred wood until the blackness had all gone. The process was repeated over and over again until the log was hollow but the sides were not too thin.

It's unlikely that the workmen did all that hard work just to make the traveller more comfortable when crossing a river, although that was one of the results. They did it, in fact, to make the boat more stable and less likely to turn over, as the centre of gravity was now so much lower. This would also mean that goods such as food, grain, and weapons could be carried. Remember that at a time when there were no roads and much of the land was covered with thick forest, a river was usually the best way of moving from one point to another.

Modern salmon fishermen using coracles

Other kinds of craft were the coracle and kayak types. These boats were made in quite a different way from the dugout canoe. Basically, each is a sort of basket covered with waterproofed skins. The water-proofing was usually done with animal fat or tar.

The builder of a coracle started by lashing osiers or birch splints together in the middle to form a sort of many-armed cross, or the spokes of a wheel. Other pieces of the same material were tied across the arms or spokes which were bent up into a bowl shape. Then the whole thing was covered with hides. The coracle was moved through the water by rotating a single paddle in a figure-of-eight motion. This took a good deal of practice if the paddler wanted to avoid going round in circles.

On the next page we'll see what middle stone age Man did with these craft.

Fishing

From the various things which have been found it is plain that some groups in this period went in for all kinds of fishing. They not only fished in lakes and rivers with hooks and nets, they also ventured out to sea and harpooned seals, porpoises and even whales.

Eel spears have turned up from time to time. Huge piles of oyster shells have come to light, showing that it was just about possible for a tribe to stay in the same place for years at a stretch and to live entirely on the products of river and sea.

Some fishing was done by one person alone; other kinds needed the co-operation of several people. 'One-man' operations included spearing, both with a single point spear with a sharpened and hardened tip and also a fork or trident with three prongs. Another way of doing the same thing was to stand quietly in shallowish water and shoot the fish with a bow and arrow, to which was attached a light line.

There was a way of catching your food without spending a long time over it. You could make a fish trap or lobster pot.

Fish spears, hooks and harpoons

Angling with a hook and line wasn't so popular but it wasn't unknown. The reason it was fairly uncommon was that it took too much time, for one hook could only catch one fish. Hooks were carved from bone or horn.

The efforts of everyone were needed when a fishing 'round-up' was to be done. A long line of people might splash out across a lake, driving the fish before them with shouts and beating the surface of the water with reed bundles. As in the old stone age, it's possible that some tribes knew how to poison a stream with the sap from trees or bushes and send the fish floating to the top of the water. We really don't know but it's quite likely that they did.

We are on firmer ground when it comes to seine netting. A seine net was long and rectangular in shape. It hung down in the water from little floats right across a stream, or even between two boats out at sea. Remains of such a net have been found in Finland. The cord was made of bast (the inner bark of a tree) and the floats of birch bark. The knots were almost identical to those in use today.

Tools and weapons

In some ways the middle stone age was a time of invention but in others, a time of decline. There were no more superb cave paintings of animals, only engravings on tools and weapons of bone and horn. It's always possible that the people of that time turned to timber for their sculpture. If they did we don't know about it, for wood hardly ever survives very long. From the art they did leave behind, it seems unlikely.

We've seen that archaeologists had to be lucky to come across wooden objects of any great age. Well, one place where they were indeed lucky was a kitchen midden site in Denmark. Kitchen middens are nothing more than huge heaps of domestic rubbish – they didn't have dustbin collections in the middle stone age. The rubbish was often discarded oyster shells and fish bones, as it was in this case. The mound of garbage showed a long occupation of the one site for it was a hundred yards long, fifty yards wide and several feet high.

The wooden object the diggers found when they came to investigate this middle stone age dump was a bow for firing arrows and was the first direct proof we have for the existence of such a weapon as early as the mesolithic period.

Spear throwers, as we've seen, were invented in the old stone age and they continued to be used in this period also. Spears and arrows were either cut to a point which was then hardened over a fire or they were tipped with tiny flint points.

Those very small flints are known as 'microliths', a Greek word meaning 'small stones'. They are very common and are found at most mesolithic sites. They were probably made by striking flakes from a flint core and then snapping them into small pieces.

Microliths were then used for one of the age's greatest inventions – the composite tool. Composite merely means that the implement was not made of one stone but several. An example of this was the saw or sickle, made by setting a lot of diamond shaped flint chips into a bone, horn or piece of wood. Microliths appeared in Europe just after 10,000 B.C. but a good deal earlier in Africa.

Microliths

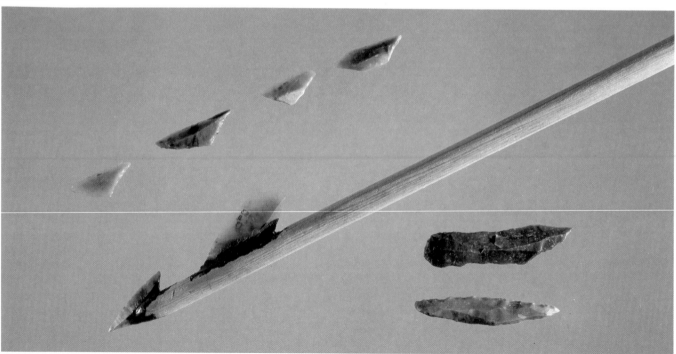

Sickle

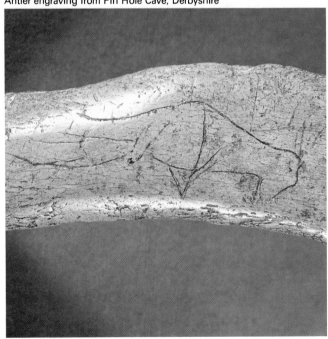

Painted pebbles from Mas d'Azil, France
Antler engraving from Pin Hole Cave, Derbyshire

Handles for tools probably date back to the end of the old stone age but they were only really fully used in the middle stone age. It's possible for us to knock in a nail with the hammer head alone but much easier if it has a handle.

We have seen how fish hooks were made of bone: harpoons with several barbs were fashioned from the antlers of red deer. Many of the weapons and tools were made of bone or horn, although stone continued to provide for a lot of Man's needs.

Types of stones which still puzzle archaeologists are the vast collections of painted pebbles discovered at Mas d'Azil in France. No one knows what the various markings on them could possibly mean, that is, if they mean anything at all. Small round pebbles were, of course, often used to crack open oyster shells. We know this because they are sometimes found inside the empty, broken shell. Unfortunately, there is no such simple explanation for these curiously marked stones.

The climate changes

How the rain belt moved from North Africa to Europe

An oasis in North Africa

As the ice disappeared towards the Arctic in Northern Europe about ten thousand years ago, the snows of winter turned mostly to rain. The rainfall on which the people, animals and plants of N. Africa and the Near East had depended for centuries gradually moved away towards Europe.

The rain did not go completely but it was much reduced. Plants die if they don't get water, and over the years the less hardy ones simply disappeared from some regions. Often it was a case of the parent bush or tree surviving for a while but whose seeds did not take root and grow owing to a lack of rain.

The grasslands of North Africa began to develop patches of bare earth where nothing could flourish: the dry heat sucked from the soil what little moisture there was, leaving it to be blown about as a fine powder. Gradually the patches grew larger and started to join up with other patches. As the centuries went by, plants could grow only where a lake, river or oasis provided the water they needed.

Animals have to drink too, so they also had to live near the water. Human beings who depended on the animals for their hunting were naturally confined to the same places.

Oases and river valleys could not support the same amounts of animal and plant life that a whole region had once provided for. There were probably fewer human beings too and for the same reasons.

42

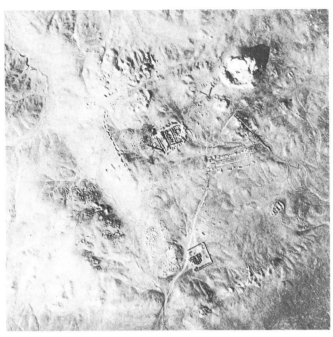
An aerial photograph showing the traces of an ancient village

In the foothills of the mountains which run from the eastern Mediterranean to the Persian Gulf, traces of villages and even small towns begin to appear. Here, in the wooded valleys, rainfall was still sufficient to support life. Many of these early settlements can be dated to around eight or nine thousand years before Christ. During the next two thousand years, many such towns were started. Their names are mostly unfamiliar to our ears – Hacilar, Catal Huyuk, Jarmo, Jericho – but they are almost certainly among the oldest towns in the world.

Here, careful burials were not unknown, often under the floors of the huts in which the people lived. Sometimes the walls of the houses were made of rammed mud, some were of stone and later on mud bricks were used. A common type of dwelling was round or square with high window spaces and no doorway at ground level. If you wanted to get in to your house, you had to climb a wooden ladder and get home by way of a smoke hole in the roof.

Food containers of wood and stone were made at first, then baskets waterproofed with animal skins or tar, if locally available. These were followed by the first pottery of clay.

Civilisation was on its way but what had brought about this tremendous change? Man had been a wanderer, hunting and gathering his food – now he had begun to settle permanently in one place. Once he had owned only what he could carry on his back: now he could own as much as he could protect in his house. On the next page we shall see what had started to alter our ancestors' way of life.

From food gathering to farming

We saw that, even back in the old stone age, human beings did not live entirely on meat. They had all kinds of nuts, seeds, and roots depending on what was in season.

Hunters probably took some of this 'gathered' food with them when they went out searching for prey. It might have consisted of several handfuls of tasty seeds in an animal skin bag slung over the shoulder. If they were unlucky and did not manage a kill, at least they wouldn't go hungry. Some of the seeds in question came most likely from the ancestors of our well-known cereals such as wheat and barley. The villages and towns mentioned on the previous page owed their existence to the fact that in their neighbourhood the cereals grew wild and in abundance.

Corn grinder

We are fairly sure that Man began to harvest the heads of these plants long before he knew how to grow them for himself. Sickles were made by setting small sharp stone chips into handles and examples have been found with plant stem scratches, still identifiable after several thousand years. If there were enough collectable seeds nearby, town life became possible.

The collection of plant seeds was one thing, the eating of them quite another! It was quickly found that grinding the seeds between two stones was better than grinding them with your teeth. The result was flour from which a kind of bread could be made. The stone grinders, or querns, have been dug up on many Near Eastern sites.

The biggest step in Man's advance was still to be taken however. This was the change over from collecting the cereals to actually growing them. How was the new idea discovered? Probably by accident. Perhaps the hunters might sit to eat their unground seeds on a fallen log. They had been unlucky in the hunt all the morning but they knew about the log from previous expeditions and they chose this as their place to eat at midday because there was also a stream nearby.

The scene may be imagined. The men and boys sit on the log and open their food bags. A few seeds are scattered as they eat. One of the hunters notices the plants growing by the log and points them out to his companions. 'There are always a lot of this sort growing here,' he says.

Of course, if he and his friends come back in a few months, some of the seeds they dropped at their picnic will have sprouted into new plants. All this is obvious to us – you sow seeds in your back garden, mark the row with a wooden peg, keep the weeds down, water the ground and up comes the plant you want. It wasn't so obvious to the people of those days. The scene round the log with the hunters and their scattered lunch had to be repeated time after time until something clicked in someone's head and the connection was made.

After that, it was a matter of putting the seeds in the earth deliberately, clearing away the unwanted vegetation and protecting the growing crop from the animals which would have eaten it until it was ready to gather.

Before planting, the weeds had to be removed and the soil loosened. This was done at first with a stout pointed stick. Such a slow process could be speeded up if two people co-operated, like this:

Eventually, a tame animal would take the place of the second person. But the taming of animals belongs on the next page.

From hunting to stock farming

In the same way that Man changed from being a gatherer to a crop farmer, he also gave up hunting and took to animal farming. It didn't happen overnight, of course. Hunting and gathering continued to be important at least in some settlements for centuries after the great switch was made. In the case of certain animals, Man found herding more efficient than hunting them. Again, the alteration in our ancestors' way of life was gradual, not dramatic.

The beasts first domesticated were sheep, goats, pigs and cattle. It probably happened like this: a tribe of hunters began to depend on two or three herds of animals to provide the meat they needed.

If the herds wandered in search of food and water, then the hunters had to move too – at least to be within striking distance of their food supply. It was a good deal easier to take animals that tend to crowd together in herds or flocks, rather than those which prefer to be on their own. In the latter case, you have only one chance of a kill but with a herd, if you miss one animal, there are plenty of others.

It took some time before Man realised he could prevent the flock from moving away and keep them in good health if only he could provide them with food and water.

He may have co-operated with his friends and relations to drive a herd of cattle into a steep ravine from which there was only one exit – the way they had gone in. The next step was to put a fence or thorn hedge across the mouth of the ravine. If they had chosen well and the valley had a stream and extensive areas of grass, the herd could be kept alive.

Driving goats into a ravine

Meat goes bad after a while, especially in a warm climate, so it was a great advantage for Man to keep live animals and to butcher one just before it was to be eaten.

Other ways in which a tame herd could have been built up were: 1. some single wild animals were captured instead of being killed, or 2. the young of some species were taken in and reared after the parents had been killed.

Other animals were also tamed or domesticated. These included not only dogs which had been helping Man to hunt since the old stone age but also goats, sheep and pigs which were, at least to begin with, solely meat animals. The idea of shearing sheep for their wool or milking cows probably came later.

Some species were eventually pressed into service as draught or riding animals. Oxen were trained to help with the ploughing and after a long while, horses were broken for use, both for hauling and riding.

Donkeys were also caught and tamed. In other parts of the world, camels, elephants, alpacas and llamas were forced to help Man's slow climb towards civilisation.

Attraction of river valleys

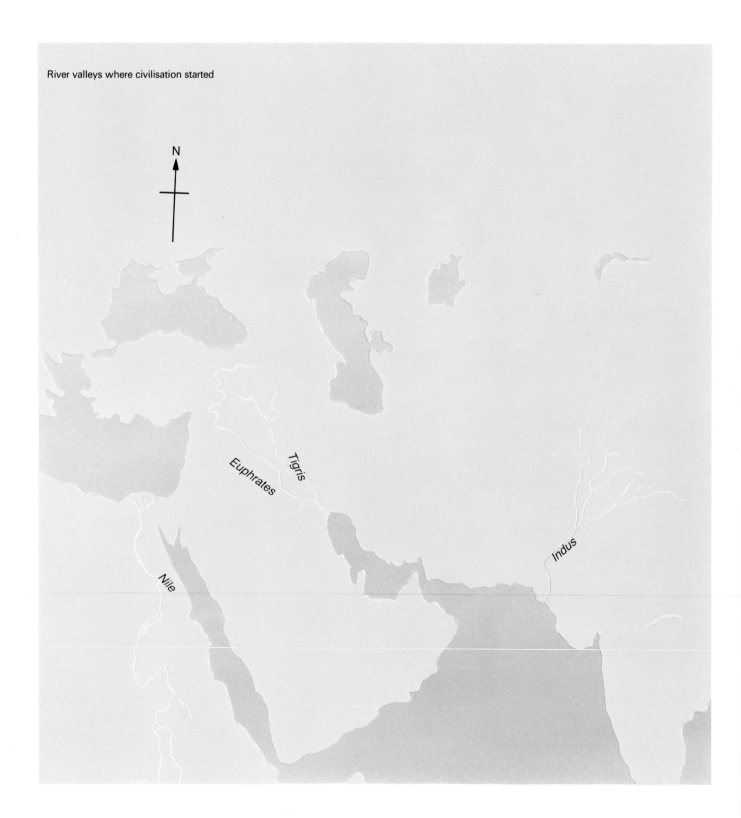

River valleys where civilisation started

Over the centuries it was gradually noticed that the great river valleys of North Africa and Asia were ideal places in which to grow food. There was plenty of water for the crops, and the weather was hot enough for the farmer to produce two, or (if he were lucky) even three harvests a year.

Another advantage was the fact that the surrounding countryside was fairly flat. With steeply sloping ground the farmer has problems. Ploughing vertically up and down the slopes is a quick way to invite the rain to wash all your soil away. Sometimes, hillsides with abrupt slopes can only be worked if a great deal of labour is spent on making terraces, or flat steps in the rising ground. None of these problems faced the river valley dweller.

The earliest settlements in the Nile valley can be dated to a period about 30,000 years ago but no one knows whether the first farmers to live in Egypt were descendants of these old stone age men or newcomers from elsewhere.

It seems certain that wild plants were harvested along the banks of the river long before anyone set out to grow them deliberately. Sickles for reaping and stones for grinding the seeds have been found. Peoples who used them couldn't at that time depend on plants entirely, or even mainly, for the food they ate. There were fish to be caught in the river and animals to be hunted.

The Nile plain was wetter and wider some 10,000 years ago than it is now and there would have been more game, particularly along the little tributary streams which fed the Nile. Nowadays they are dry watercourses or wadis, with no wild animals to hunt.

We know for sure that these early settlers used stone-tipped spears and arrows, many of which have been found in modern times. Their existence proves that the tribesmen of those days still depended on hunting for much of their living.

However, river valley farming was beginning to provide a growing share of what they ate. There was another advantage to this sort of life. The soil was easily worked and there was a large area which could be cultivated.

In the early days of farming up in the foothill valleys of the northern mountains, a family would have to move every few years because the soil was exhausted. It was far easier to find a place to settle in the great river valleys of the Nile, Tigris-Euphrates and the Indus. And, of course, once you were there, you could stay as long as you liked, for the soil never became exhausted. You'll find out why on the next page.

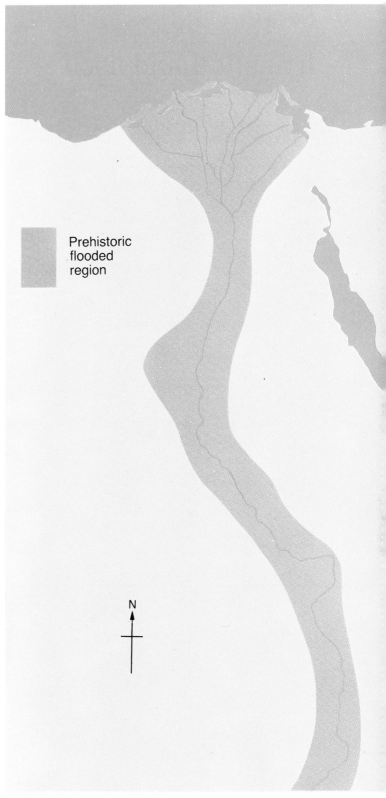

Prehistoric flooded region

Prehistoric flooded region of the Nile

N

Irrigation and flood

In all the great river valleys where early civilisations started, there were periods of the year when the water levels began to rise until the rivers overflowed. This was particularly noticeable in the Nile valley. In Egypt there was just one great annual flood – not a series of minor, irritating ones.

The Nile is the longest river in the world and rises far to the south. Spring rains and snow melting from mountain tops thousands of miles from the sea flow down into the lakes and streams which feed the Nile.

The water level rises slowly and travels – just as slowly – down to the Mediterranean. The flood water spills over the banks on both sides – sometimes hundreds of yards to right and left.

The waters scour the hillsides and stream beds, picking up a great deal of mud – so much that the colour of the river changes from green to brownish red. By mid-summer, the swollen Nile has spread out over the fields bordering it. The farmers wait anxiously for the waters to go down.

Diagram showing the variation of the height of the River Nile during the year

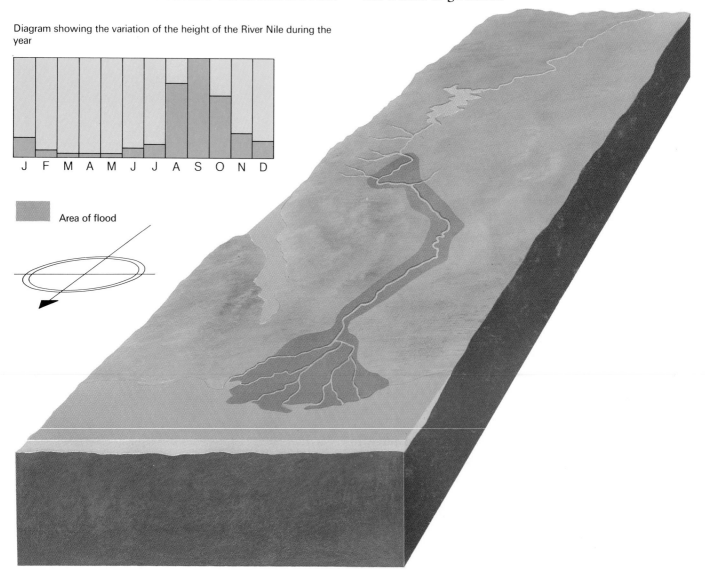

J F M A M J J A S O N D

Area of flood

When the land emerges once more into the light and air, the peasants can see that their farms and small holdings are thickly plastered with fertile mud. Now we can see why, in the Nile valley, the soil is never exhausted and why farmers don't have to move on to a better site every few years.

Every mid-September the level starts to drop and when the river has returned to its normal course, the farmer sets out to plough or hoe his fields. Provided he doesn't let the mud dry to a hard crust in the hot sun, not too much effort is needed to get the soil ready. When it is, the seeds of rye, wheat, barley, peas or beans are scattered on the sticky mud.

The next step is to drive the sheep or goats over the fields, their hooves burying the seed and covering it up. Of course, the baking sun sends the shade temperature up to over 100 degrees fahrenheit, so it doesn't do to allow the ground to dry out completely, or the plants would wither and die.

Somehow or other the farmer has to find a way of watering his growing crops. One method is to irrigate his fields. He must dig out small channels all over his land and arrange them so that they slope down away from the river.

Unluckily, by the time the flood is over, the Nile is probably many feet below the level of his farm, so he has to use a machine to get the water up. This is called a shaduf: the water bucket is on one end and the other is plastered with clay to balance it. The farmer dips the bucket on its rope down into the Nile and uses the counterweight to lift the water to the right level. When the bucket is just above the earth bank, the farmer swivels it round and tips it into the channel that supplies his crops.

A shaduf

Raising water using an Archimedes screw

The rise of the leaders

In most of the early civilisations, leaders arose naturally – they usually do. Even a small group of people will normally split up into the leader and the led.

This was important in Egypt, Sumer and ancient Pakistan – particularly in the first mentioned. It was vital for the farmers to grow as much food as they could, so as large an area as possible was cultivated.

To irrigate the largest farms, long and deep water channels were needed. It was all very well for a peasant and his family to scrape shallow ditches through the dirt of his small-holding but for a canal which had to reach to the farthest limit of a great estate, many men had to be employed.

This meant dividing them up into gangs, giving out tasks and getting them to work together. Those who gave the orders were the ones who seemed to know what was to be done and how to do it. One way of becoming a leader was to show that you knew things that the others didn't. For example a man who was able to foretell the coming of the annual flood would be very important indeed. It's all very well to say, 'The Nile floods once a year, so it's easy to say when it will be.' The difficulty is that although *we* know there are just over 365 days in a year, the earliest settlers didn't.

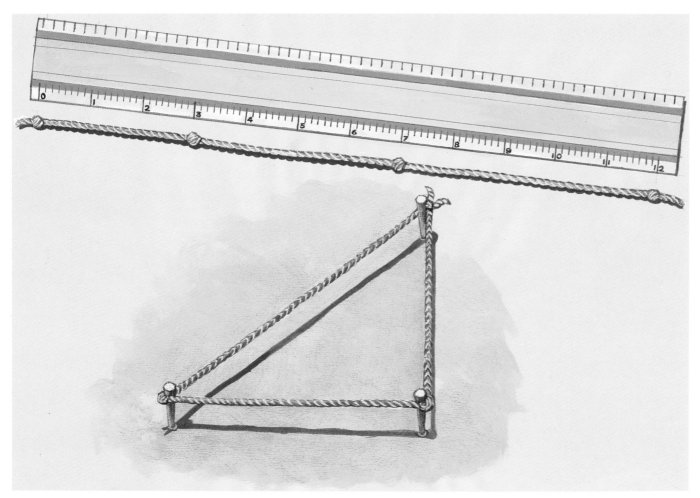

How to make a right angle with a piece of knotted string

How would you go about calculating the number of days in a year? It isn't as simple as it sounds – you can't just count because you don't know where to stop. The cleverest of the Egyptians worked it out by noting the position of the star Sirius in the sky and waiting until it came back again to that same position.

When the floods went down, a new problem appeared – where exactly was each peasant's farm? You couldn't mark the boundaries in the dry season, for such markers would have been swept away by the rising river waters.

It was left to those who could do the proper calculations to give each farming family the same amount of land as before. Another kind of calculation had to be made when civilisation really began: the designing of large public and royal buildings such as temples, granaries, palaces and tombs. It's surprising how hard it is to lay out the corner of a building so that it forms a right angle. You can't use the corner of a book or anything like it, as there wasn't, at that time, anything like it at all.

We don't know how, when or by whom the problem was solved but a method was hit upon. All we can do is guess that the river valley people used the string and pegs method.

If you make sure that the string is stretched and the three pegs positioned so that the tight cord between them measures three, four and five units (inches, footlengths – whatever you like) thus forming a triangle, you get an almost exact right angle.

All these sorts of tasks needed brain, rather than muscle power and they also required some method of recording, or writing things down. Ways of doing this varied from place to place and we'll look at how it was done later.

The men who could count, calculate, and set down their results for others to read had an edge over their neighbours. If they could work out how many men should be told off to dig a ditch, where it should run, what food each gang would need and how many bags of corn each peasant should be taxed to pay for everything, they would be looked up to as leaders – not only wise men but magicians. They were the first priests, rulers and kings.

Section 5 *Sumer*

The first settlers

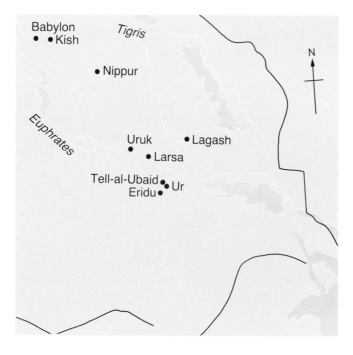

This is 'The Land Between the Rivers'. 'Mesopotamia' is what the Greeks called it. Iraq is its modern name. It – or parts of it – has had all kinds of names throughout thousands of years – Sumer, Shinar, Chaldea, Akkad, Assyria, and Babylonia are some of them.

Sumer is the name given to the earliest settled part – the area just inland from where the rivers Tigris and Euphrates empty their waters into the Persian Gulf.

Sumer can't have been a very attractive place for colonists and yet it was almost certainly here that civilisation first appeared in the world.

The rivers didn't always flood at exactly the same time each year. The floods were therefore not predictable – neither as to the time they could be expected nor as to the height of the water. It was quite a common happening for the flood to be so great that when it went down again the river had changed course.

There was little in the way of local building stone, so the first huts the people had were probably small round ones made of plaited and thatched reeds. As long as none of the peasant's family or animals had drowned in the flood, his hut could be quickly rebuilt and the outcome was not the disaster it might have been.

Modern Marsh Arab huts

Mesopotamian dairy scene

There were plenty of reeds and cane brakes but very few trees. There was desert land which needed irrigation and marshes which had to be drained. Above all there was the cruelly high summer temperature which often topped 100° fahrenheit.

Why then was the area settled at all? We can't give hard and fast reasons but we think it may have been on account of population pressure. In the mountain and hill valleys to the north and east of Sumer, people were running short of enough good farmland to feed all the extra children there were in the tribe. At least some of the families had to move on or go short of food for the rest of their lives.

We can imagine them packing up all they owned and strapping their bundles on to the backs of the donkeys they had tamed. The cattle, sheep and goats would be herded along the tracks and kept on the right path by the children helped by their dogs.

The travellers would have to live on the grain they took with them, at the same time saving enough barley and wheat seeds to sow once they got down to the river lowlands. They must also have carried dates both to eat and to plant for fresh date palm groves when they arrived in their new homeland.

The first sowing of seed was quite likely done as a ceremony with prayers to the gods of harvest, river, and weather.

Rainfall was too low to ensure the growth of the crops without some help, so every member of the family had to carry pots of water to the rows of plants in the fields. Everyone in this case meant the peasant, his wives and children, his brothers and their wives and children and even his own parents if they were not too old and feeble. They also had to join together to dig permanent irrigation ditches. By the time all the round, reed huts had been put up, there were the beginnings of a small village.

One huge advantage of being a farmer was that you had plenty of time to do other things while you were waiting for the grain to ripen. A man who hunted for a living found that it was a full time occupation and that he had very little leisure for anything else.

Pottery could be made to replace any that had been broken on the journey south. More elaborate and beautiful work could be done than was possible in a non-farming community. All kinds of storage jars, beakers, plates and dishes were fired in open, brushwood furnaces and decorated with patterns in black, brown, red and cream.

We don't know what the people called themselves and we have no idea of the language they spoke. All we know is that, with the exception of scattered towns such as Jericho, they were laying the foundations for the oldest civilisation on earth.

Halaf pottery sherds

The useful date palm

In the last section we mentioned the fact that the first settlers of Sumer had taken dates to plant in their new homeland. The date palm, according to ancient writings, had over 300 different uses. It's difficult to see how that figure was arrived at – the actual total is probably much lower. Let's see what this settler thinks about his date trees.

The peasant smiles, wipes the sweat from his brow with the back of his hand and invites us to sit down in his 'orchard'. As we settle our backs against a sturdy tree trunk, he smiles even more broadly.

'You see, he says, 'you've found out one of its advantages straight away. Without the broad leaves of the palm, there would be no shade at all in this land – and that would be hard to bear, for in summer it gets as hot as an oven. If it wasn't for the very fertile soil, I don't think anyone would actually choose to live here.'

He hands us some dates to nibble. 'Here is another of the tree's gifts – its fruit. Do you know that you could live off dates plus a bit of the fresh fronds at the top of the palm? Not that you'd want to; it'd get pretty boring, having the same thing for every meal. But you could if you had to.

'Then again, you can press the dates and squeeze out the juice. It makes a nice, refreshing drink. Or if you wanted to you could leave it to ferment and turn it into wine. That's nice too, but you shouldn't have too much, particularly if you've got to work afterwards. It's better to take some in the cool of the evening. It's not much fun hoeing a field with a dry mouth and a splitting headache, which is what you get if you drink too much of it.

'Now then, if you leave the wine in the open air for some time, it goes sour but you can still use it. You sprinkle it on your young palm leaf salad. We just call it "sour wine" – do you know what I mean?'

'Yes,' we say, 'our word is vinegar and that means "sour wine" too.'

The peasant nods approvingly and goes on with his list of good things the date palm gives him.

'You can collect the dry stones, or fruit pips, until you have two or three large bags full of them. You pile them into a heap and light a fire at one side of it. When it's going well, you cover up the fire with wet earth or clay, just leaving a little hole here and there. After a few hours the stones aren't burnt, they're cooked and you've got (for just a few hours' work) a half bag of charcoal. Marvellous stuff for cooking.

'Now, what else? Well, you can always make a string or rope from the fibre. You can pick a leaf and use it as a hat or a sunshade. You can take the main rib out of a leaf and make some kinds of furniture. You tie several of them together in whatever pattern you like. Of course there's better furniture to be had from the trunk itself. When the tree is old and past its best years of fruit bearing, it's chopped down and turned into tables, chairs, boats or even firewood.

'You could make moulds for mud bricks, or fish and wild fowl traps, or you could—'

'Thank you very much, 'we say,' you've given us quite a lot to think about.

Date cluster on a tree   Dates

Section 5 *Sumer*

Nam-sha learns to read and write

'Oh, no,' says Nam-sha, when we ask him, 'not everybody learns to read and write – only the ones the gods pick. There aren't very many scribes and you have to work hard to become one. The course lasts about twelve years. A boy is roughly eight years old when he begins but he's a man of twenty when he finishes.

'I've been doing it for four years now but my teachers keep telling me that I still don't know very much. I suppose that's true: the only things I can read are very simple tablets.'

'Tablets?'

'Yes, that's what we write on – tablets of soft, damp clay. We use reeds to make the marks. Like this,' he says, picking up a flat lump of clay.

'If you try to draw what you want to say – a picture of a hand, a tree, a foot perhaps, it gets harder to pull the reed through the surface and bits of clay twist up in front like the bow wave of a boat on the river Tigris. So we don't just draw, we use the end of the pen to stab little marks like this:

Babylonian clay tablets

It still looks like the picture of the thing you wanted to put down but over the years it gradually gets altered. We start, say, with a man's head: [sign] Done in 'print marks', it probably looked like this: [sign] Then it got turned on its side: [sign] Finally, it wound up as: [sign] You can't recognise it straight away now, not unless you know what it is.'

'Does this mean you have to learn a new sign for every new word?'

'Not quite but pretty nearly. There are tens of thousands of words in our language and it's fine if you can draw the word you need, such as 'palm tree' or 'house' but how do you draw 'fright' or 'greed'? Oh, I know you could sketch a person who is frightened or greedy but that's hard to do just with these stab marks.'

'How do you manage then?'

'Well, one sign often does duty for several words; a foot [sign] might mean 'foot' or 'kick' or 'stand' or 'measure'. On the other hand, there are over thirty different signs for 'sheep'. You can also have signs standings for parts of words and that's helps a lot.'

'Oh, yes, I know – you could draw [sign] [sign] for 'bee, leaf' (belief) which would be hard to draw otherwise.'

'That's the idea,' says Nam-sha, 'Are you scribes too?'

We look a little bit embarrassed. 'Well,' we say, hesitating a little, 'we *can* read and write but only in our own language, not yours'.

'Does it take a long time to read in your foreign tongue?' asks Nam-sha.

'No,' we say, 'not nearly as long as it does in the Land of the Two Rivers. You see, we have only 26 signs to learn – one for each sound. Well, almost like that. We call our collection of signs an alphabet.'

'We don't have an alphabet,' says Nam-sha, 'I don't think it would work.'

'How did writing start?' we want to know.

'No one is sure. I asked my teachers and they said it was given to Man by the gods. But I think it started with the temples rather than the gods.'

'How so?'

'Well, in the beginning, those who ran the big farms and large estates (which mostly belonged to the temples anyway) had to have some way of helping their memory.

'If you have to remember what amounts of fish, meat and grain you produced last year and how much had to be collected from each peasant and how much given to each servant and workman – it just gets too much. It's so much easier to draw a picture of an ear of grain [sign] or an ox head [sign] and to add strokes to show how much of a thing. Then you could put a different sign for each man who paid taxes or was paid wages. It sounds complicated but it isn't. Those doing the note taking probably wrote on slabs of stone to start with but clay is easier to find, it's cheaper and there's a lot more of it.'

Nam-sha is right. The Land of the Two Rivers is built of clay. Of course, the clay tablets might have lost their picture words after twenty or thirty centuries but luckily for us some survived. Important tablets were sometimes baked deliberately to preserve them. Quite a few burnt in accidental temple and palace fires. Thus the words were fixed for ever.

Section 5 *Sumer*

Clay bricks and buildings

House building in Sumer

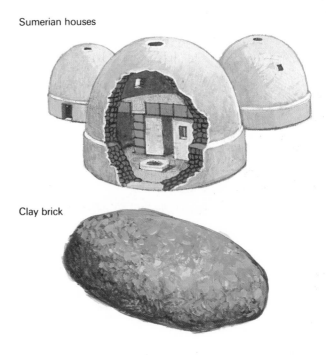

Sumerian houses

Clay brick

Gradually, as scientists have dug into the mounds of ruins in Sumer and elsewhere in the valley of the Two Rivers, enough clay tablets have been found to rough out a sketchy outline of Sumerian history.

No one king ruled over the entire area. On the contrary, in early times, each city was independent of the others. The local king or priest/king ruled an area around his own stronghold.

At the beginning of written history, about 5,000 years ago, Sumer was governed in this way but as the centuries passed, other peoples overran the area. There were the Akkadians and they in their turn were conquered by the Amorites or Babylonians. The conquest of the latter by the Assyrians takes us to only a few centuries before the Christian era. The last people to subdue the area before the time of Christ were the Persians.

Buildings changed with the years and so did the bricks from which they were made. Originally, settlers may simply have used handfuls of wet clay to make a crude wall, keeping the mounds of mud from toppling over by one of two methods. The peasant might outline his house's shape with lumps of clay which he then allowed to dry in the hot sun. Further handfuls were placed on top and heat hardened in their turn.

This was a very slow method if you had to wait hours for each course to dry out. A simpler way was to use timber shuttering and ram or stamp the clay down between the boards.

Later still, bricks were invented. The first Sumerian bricks were very oddly shaped. The worker took a double handful of clay and rolled it roughly into a shape like a small marrow. Then he slightly flattened top, bottom and sides. After this, workers took square wooden frames which they filled with a clay, sand and straw mixture. Then the frame was lifted off and the whole process was repeated. Long rows of bricks were allowed to harden in the sun; only if they were to be used in a place where they needed to be waterproof were they baked in a kiln or brick oven. It wasn't until civilisation was well established that bricks were made absolutely square with flat, even faces.

The colour of the bricks was determined by the colour of the clay from which they were made, varying through yellow, brown, red, grey or even black. If this was thought to be a bit dull, lines of coloured clay cones were pressed into wet clay walls in patterns.

The bricks were stuck together with wet mud or bitumen, a tar-like substance which will not let water through. Bitumen occurs naturally in parts of the Middle East, oozing up from the ground.

In earliest times, the only buildings made of brick were public ones – temples, palaces, or granaries. The temple was a shrine to a local or more widely worshipped deity.

Quite often the people did not start a new temple elsewhere when their present one was destroyed or it wore out. They filled in the empty spaces with brick rubble or clay and then built a new temple on top of it. Thus as the years went by, the temple mound grew larger, taller, wider and longer with the remains of a dozen or perhaps even twenty earlier temples buried inside it.

Some of the largest of these are known as 'ziggurats'. They are faintly similar in size and shape to the pyramids of Egypt but were never used as burial places. Moreover, the wide, flat terraces were often planted with flowers, bushes and even trees. From this custom comes the story of one of the seven wonders of the world, 'The Hanging Gardens of Babylon'. It must have been very pleasant for the priests who served the god to be able to sit out in the shade of some large tree in a land famous for its searingly hot summers. It can't have been much fun for the gardeners, though. They had to haul up the water needed by the vegetation. It's surprising the vast number of gallons required each day by even a modest sized tree.

If a building isn't kept in good repair, it gradually crumbles. This true of almost any building, even stone ones, given enough time. For those made of mud brick, the process was quicker. Once the repairs stopped, the passing years saw the ziggurat collapse on itself like a weak blancmange or jelly. Weeds grew on the crumbling brick. What had been a proud temple now looked like a low hill standing in the desert.

The modern Arabs that live there call such a hill a 'tell'. It took a great deal of digging in the 19th century to prove that these hummocky tells were really the remains of a great civilisation.

Ziggurat in ruins at Uruk

Rebuilt ziggurat

Section 5 *Sumer*

Gods and heroes

It is sometimes difficult to say who was a god and who was a hero in the Land of the Two Rivers. Because facts are rather scarce for the very early periods, a number of beings could have been either or even both at once.

The Sumerians had very many gods. Some, such as En-lil or Marduk, were worshipped, at one time or another, all over the area. Others were venerated in only one town or village – for example, the worshippers of Shara were to be found at Umma alone.

Every single place had its patron god, and there were heavenly beings who looked after all parts of

Gudea

The Goddess of Earth

earthly life. Ashnan was in charge of the barley fields, Shumu-qan looked after cattle, and the goddess Gula protected mothers-to-be.

The countrywide gods included An, chief of the gods, the moon god Nanna and his child, the sun god, Utu. There was Ninurta who protected warriors, Pasag, who did the same for travellers, Inanna, the goddess of love and Dumuzi, her husband. Enki was the god of life-giving waters.

It was thought that the land of Sumer belonged to the gods, and the priests carried out their wishes. Everyone was expected to sing hymns, say prayers, make sacrifices and bring offerings to the local temple. This might be a wayside shrine, an altar at the corner of a city street, or it could even be one of the gigantic ziggurats mentioned on the previous page.

Gods could be annoyed at what you did and punish you, or they could be pleased and reward you. There were so many of these heavenly beings that the average Sumerian's life was totally hedged about with religion – or perhaps we should call it superstition.

Once a year, particularly in later times at places such as the city of Babylon, the new year festival (called Akitu) was held. It celebrated the sacred marriage of the gods plus the anniversary, both of the creation of the world and also the present king's reign.

There were many creation myths. Some resembled those told in the Old Testament of the Bible. Perhaps the most striking resemblence between the religions of Sumer and that of the ancient Hebrews is the story of the heroic god-king, Gilgamesh.

Gilgamesh was the fifth king of Uruk, an early Sumerian city. Saddened by the death of a friend, he learned of a holy man named Ut-napishtim who, rumour had it, would never die. Gilgamesh resolved to find out his secret.

Gilgamesh is often described as a cross between Hercules and Ulysses, a bearded strong man, brave as a lion who would fight any man (or wild animal) and win.

After many adventures, Gilgamesh finally met Ut-napishtim and begged for his secret. The latter told him this story.

'Mankind had become so sinful, that the gods, especially En-lil, made up their minds to destroy human beings utterly, by means of a great flood. But Ea, one of the gods, secretly took pity on us. One night as I lay half awake, a voice spoke to me through the thin wall of my reed hut.

'The voice advised me to tear down the hut, forget my possessions and build a ship big enough to take not only me, my wife and family and all my workmen and their families but also examples of every living thing. I did all I was bidden. When I had finished the ship, I loaded it up with gold and silver and sat down to wait.

'It wasn't long before the clouds piled up in the sky and the first raindrops began to fall. The human beings and animals came aboard and I closed all the doors and windows. The worst storm ever known then broke and my ship was soon afloat. It rained as hard as you can imagine for six days and nights.

'On the seventh day the rain eased off, so I opened a window. We were alone on an empty sea but before long we settled gently on a half submerged rock. I found out later that it was the top of what had been Mount Nisir.

'I sent out a dove but she came back. A week later I sent out a swallow but she also returned. Another seven days passed before I released a raven which did not come back to us. This meant that the waters were going down, so we landed on the island mountain top and burned a sacrificial offering of sweet cane, myrtle and cedar.

'The gods smelled the smoke and came to look. En-lil was angry that he had been disobeyed and he blamed Ea for warning me. But Ea spoke so warmly of mankind that En-lil's heart was melted. He blessed me and gave my wife and me the gift of everlasting life.'

Then was Gilgamesh sad; for immortality was not a secret to be learned but a gift of the gods.

Section 5 *Sumer*

Houses and everyday life

At the dawn of Sumer's history, families moving to the south of the country often lived in houses made of bundles of reeds. Naturally, none of these has survived but we have a fair idea of what they looked like from clay tablet pictures and descriptions. Even today, some of the people who inhabit parts of the marshy south still live in similar huts. (see page 54).

Farther north on a tributary of the River Tigris, archaeologists have dug out a village called Jarmo. The houses there were made of rammed clay. Bricks had not been invented at that time, some eight or nine thousand years ago. Later on in Jarmo, stone foundations were laid before the walls were set up. Roofs were thatched with reeds and plastered with clay.

Each house had several rooms, none of which was more than about six feet in length. In some, a hole had been scooped out in the floor and lined with clay. These were the first direct evidence of a cooking device mentioned on page 27. The cook dropped hot stones into the hole after filling it with water, thus boiling whatever food was also put in.

Possibly only about 150 people lived there but Jarmo is one of the earliest villages known to be dependent on farming rather than hunting.

Jarmo

Among the crops they grew were kinds of wheat and barley, peas and lentils. The only farm animal was the goat: if the villagers wanted the meat of pigs, sheep or cattle, they still had to hunt them. It seems from the enormous number of snail shells that these creatures must have been on the menu too.

Even after the invention of writing some 5,000 years ago and the development of cities such as Ur, Eridu, Lagash and Uruk, the bulk of the population still earned their living from animal and crop farming. Barley, wheat and millet were staple crops, the grain being used for porridge, bread or beer. Peas and lentils were grown as were onions and garlic, leeks and melons, cucumbers and lettuce, watercress and spices. Sesame was planted for the oil it yielded – oil which must have been used for cooking and lighting.

Among the fruits the Sumerians enjoyed were apples, peaches, cherries, plums and (of course) the very useful date. Apart from bread, fruit, vegetables and some meat, Sumerians seem to have eaten a lot of cheese. In addition, the rivers and sea abounded with fish and there were always birds such as ducks and geese to be snared.

About 4,000 years ago, the houses took on a pattern that was to survive in the Middle East right to the present day. Let us visit the ancient town of Ur in 2,000 B.C., probably at the same time and place that Abraham was born. Here is a man named Ruk-shin who will take us to see what his house is like.

He beckons us away from the granaries, huge temples and public buildings to a narrow street running southward. In fact, all the streets are narrow – so much so that carts could not get through them. Even a laden donkey would cause us to press ourselves against the windowless walls.

'Just along here,' our guide says, 'I must go to the market to buy a jug for my wife.' We walk down another narrow street which widens out into a small square. The shops are mostly one, two or three roomed buildings with storerooms or workplaces at the back. On the street side goods are spread out for sale on stalls both inside and outside the shop. Awnings of woven reeds give welcome shade to most of the businesses.

Street scene

Cooking

A colourful scene meets our eyes in the square. Amid the salesmen crying their wares of food, clothes, spices, and earthenware there are street musicians, entertainers, jugglers and acrobats. There are pedlars, water sellers, writers of letters for those who can't do it for themselves – and even a story teller with a small audience hanging on his every word.

Ruk-shin has got his jug and leads us on to his house. 'In here,' he says, opening a small wooden door for us. We step through and immediately notice how much cooler it is in the interior courtyard. We wash the street dust off of our feet and pour the water away down a central drain which also helps carry flood water away when the river rises. Ruk-shin made sure that the lower brick courses of his house were kiln fired and thus waterproofed. Higher up where the floods cannot reach, sun-dried bricks will do.

The lime-washed walls rise to a narrow gallery supported on wooden beams. This divides the house in two – the upper part for the family's private rooms and the lower for the kitchen, work and storerooms and the room for entertaining guests. This latter is a long, narrow room with seating all the way round three sides. It is very like what is seen in a modern Arab house. There are a couple of small tables and many cushions and rugs.

Also on the ground floor is a courtyard partly roofed over. Here are Ruk-shin's household gods. The statuettes in the little chapel are the family's 'guardian angels'. The chapel is not only a place of worship, it is a burial vault too. There is a tomb below the brick floor where Ruk-shin's dead ancestors lie. Many years before, the dead had been buried in separate cemeteries, well away from town but this is no longer the custom and the ancestors are nearby where the family can pray to them and involve them in the life of Ruk-shin and his relations.

We say goodbye to our guide at his door and make our way down the street. We notice that although most of the houses seem to show a modest prosperity, there are poor families living in half ruined houses, or even in lean-to shacks.

Section 5 *Sumer*

Conquerors and kings

Babylonian soldier

Sargon's head

Here's a soldier we can ask about the great rulers in his part of Mesopotamia. He agrees to talk to us but has never heard the word 'Mesopotamia'. We have to explain that although we call the area 'Iraq', the earlier name comes from Greek words meaning 'Middle of the Rivers'. The name isn't earlier to the soldier: it is Greek and he has never heard of the Greeks or their language. For him they don't yet exist and his description of the valleys of the Tigris and Euphrates are the words 'Sumer' for the south and 'Akkad' for the central region.

By our reckoning it is 1740 B.C. but of course our soldier hasn't heard of Christ either so he calls the year the 52nd of the reign of Hammurabi.

'Who was the greatest conqueror?' we ask.

'I suppose that must be Hammurabi, our present king. Mind you, the first great conqueror in the world ruled in Akkad more than 500 years ago.'

'Who was that?'

'He was called Sargon. No one knows much about his early life. We think he was the son of a shepherd up river – near where the tributary Khabur joins the Euphrates. He got a job in the local king's palace and rose to be cup bearer to the king of Kish. What happened next is a mystery: the next thing we know is that he's become king himself.

'Shortly after that, he reorganised the army. Before his time, a king had only a few full time soldiers but Sargon reckoned to be able to muster 5,000 fully armed professional fighting men whenever he wanted to. When he planned an attack on a neighbouring kingdom, he made army service compulsory for hundreds of thousands of young men.

'A king's normal bodyguard had uniform helmets and spears and attacked behind lines of shields. In fact the whole army had tended to advance in that sort of formation. A phalanx, they called it.

'Sargon made many alterations to battle tactics. He broke up the phalanx and armed the infantry with bows and battle axes. Then he had some battle wagons made – little four wheeled carts drawn by four onagers, or wild asses. Each one had a driver and a warrior wielding a battle axe and hurling spears from a large sheaf. They were neither manoeuvrable nor fast enough to deserve the name 'chariot' but they were good for medium and close range fighting.

'Sargon used his new army to carve out a larger kingdom for himself by conquering neighbouring kings. Then he moved south and struck at the Sumerian cities of the plains. When he captured Uruk he had the walls smashed and took its king, Lugalzagesi a prisoner in chains. Then he attacked north westward towards the Great Sea* and the mountains of Lebanon and Turkey.

'Eastward, he beat the Elamites and the men of Assur—'

'I think we call that Assyria.'

'He forced open trade routes to every nation round about and even down to the coast of Africa. It's said he carried out his conquests because of a need to get stone, gold, silver, copper, tin and even timber but that's only half the story. I believe he conquered because he was made that way – some men are.

'He reigned 56 years and boasted that his empire would last for a thousand. But his descendants let it fall to pieces and the last of his line died out less than two centuries later.'

'What about Hammurabi?

'Our present king? Oh, yes, there's a lot of similarities between Sargon and him. He didn't come from a humble family of course – his father was already king of Babylon. Our city wasn't as big, as important or as beautiful as it is now: after all, his kingdom was only a strip of land about 40 miles up river and the same distance down, with a width of no more than 20 miles. All around us were larger and more powerful kingdoms.

'Hammurabi prepared the army for five years before trying his strength. Then he struck in three directions at once – up river, down river and eastward across the Tigris towards the mountains.

'All was successful and the next twenty years were spent in making an empire out of his conquests. But in the 29th year of his reign, we were attacked by a huge army made up of most of the enemies we had fought against. Praise to the Gods! We won an enormous victory. The following year, the priests who told fortunes from the livers of animals told him that the signs were favourable, so we attacked – again in all directions. Again we were successful and by about 14 years ago, we Babylonians owned the whole area from the gulf up to Assyria. Now Hammurabi can call himself "King of the four quarters of the world."'

*The Mediterranean

Battle scene

Law givers

The stele of Hammurabi from the Louvre, Paris

Our soldier is still willing to talk to us about Babylon so we ask about the system of laws his king has set down. 'Come with me,' he says and we walk some distance until we come into the courtyard of a temple where there is a round stone pillar, or stele, about eight feet high. It is covered with hundreds of lines of Babylonian writing, or cuneiform, and has a picture carved in the stone of Hammurabi praying to Marduk, the chief god and god of the sun and of justice.

'You see,' says our informant, 'you know now what a great military man Hammurabi is. What you don't know is what a good king he is too. He runs the empire

very well and has made our city of Babylon stronger and more beautiful than it has ever been.

'He has also set out the laws which we must all obey. They were written on clay tablets at first. Now they are carved into pillars of black stone and are set up in temple courtyards for everyone to see all over the land.'

'But can everyone read these laws?'

'No, they cannot. I can't read myself but I have been told what they are.'

'Could you tell us, then? We can't read Babylonian either.'

'Certainly. As much as I can remember. To start with, you've seen this picture of our king? Underneath that, there are a few sentences about who he is, what the laws are and how everyone must obey them. Then it explains how justice must be done. You know, punishment for someone telling lies at a trial, or the throwing out of a judge proved to have taken a bribe.

'You realise that all these laws haven't been invented by Hammurabi? Many are what you would call common law – that is to say, a law may be written down but it's only something that has always been done, written or not. In any case, Hammurabi wasn't the first ruler to lay out a complete set of laws; other kings have done the same thing, I'm told – for example, Ur-nammu, ruler of Sumer and Akkad nearly four centuries ago. Then there was Lipit-Ishtar, who lived about two hundred years ago – and many others.

'There are 282 laws all told. The biggest section deals with family problems – you know, marriage and the duties of husbands and wives, desertion, adoption, inheritance, divorce and so on.

'The next group is to do with land. That is to say, laws dealing with trespass, rent, land use and the rights and responsibilities of landlords and tenants.

'The third group is about business and trade – matters such as what people owe, what to do with someone who runs off with something they've been trusted with, rates of interest and things like that.

'Then there's the criminal law – how to keep crime down, punishments for theft, robbery and attacks on the person.'

'Ah! "muggings"! So you have them too?'

'I don't know if you'd include this in the list of mutilations but if you tell lies about someone's wife you could have half your hair cut off.'

'You must be joking!'

'I'm a soldier. I wouldn't joke about things like that. In fact there are other laws that probably sound just as strange to you. If it can be proved that you've hit your elder brother, disowned your parents, or kicked your mother, you can be made a slave.

'Mind you, not all the laws are like this: there are rules about business, lots of them – you know, rates of pay, the rate for hiring a cart or a boat and all sorts of other everyday things.'

'A great man, your Hammurabi.'

'Well, we think so.'

Hammurabi

'Of course we do. And the single biggest change the king has brought in here is the severer penalties for this kind of crime. In the old days, most gentlemen could settle a matter like this by paying a fine. Well, we've still got fines but there are all sorts of punishments nowadays. The death penalty operates for housebreaking, being a brigand or a witch, kidnapping, receiving stolen property and even telling lies in some kinds of court cases.'

'How are death sentences carried out?'

'Oh, they might be tied up and thrown in the river, or killed with a sharp implement, or even burned.'

'That sounds pretty horrible.'

'Some might say it was better to be dead than mutilated.'

'Mutilated?'

'Oh, yes. If you put someone's eye out, you get your own eye put out. If you break someone's arm or leg, the same thing happens to you. Actually this could happen even if you meant no harm. For instance, if you were a doctor and you operated on someone carelessly and they lost an eye or a limb – well you know what would happen: you could lose your own eye or have a hand cut off.

Section 5 *Sumer*

The royal tombs at Ur

Archaeologists learn a lot from ancient graves, particularly when it was thought a dead person would need his earthly possessions in the afterlife and they were buried with him. For this reason, Sir Leonard Woolley was delighted to have come across what have come to be known as 'The Royal Tombs at Ur'. Ur, you may remember was the birth-place of Abraham.

From 1926 onward Sir Leonard dug a number of two month seasons, during which he turned up some 450 graves. One has become famous as 'The Death Pit of Ur', a description given it by Woolley himself.

When the earth had been carefully removed from the large, oblong hole, a gruesome sight was revealed. One corner of the grave had a sizable limestone-walled tomb built into it but on the floor of the pit were 74 human skeletons. Some of them had jewellery scattered about the bones – for example, silver and gold hair ribbons and many semi-precious stones.

There were other interesting finds, including the remains of what turned out to be harps and a statue of a ram caught in a thicket, reminiscent of the Bible story about Abraham and Isaac.

To begin with, the archaeologists were puzzled. It wasn't easy to reconstruct the events leading up to the funeral just from the remains of bodies and objects which had lain underground for well over 4,000 years. Sir Leonard Woolley himself gave this version of what might have happened.

'The royal funeral in the limestone tomb was completed when the workmen filled in the doorway with bricks and stone and added a top coat of plaster.

'In the opposite corner of the pit, an earth ramp leads down from the ground surface. Moving slowly downwards, a solemn procession walks along the ramp, lower and lower into the grave. These are the human sacrifices – members of the royal court, both men and women – servants, courtiers, soldiers and grooms. Each one is dressed in his or her best garments, the women with headdresses of precious metal foil, plus carnelian and lapis lazuli jewels. One woman must have overslept and is a little late for the ceremony, for at her side (possibly in a long rotted pocket) was a roll of silver foil which ought to have been in her hair. (When *we* say 'silver foil' we mean a thin sheet of silver coloured metal of a cheap kind: in the death pit it was real silver).

'Then come the musicians with their harps and cymbals followed by the ass- and ox-drawn chariots, the animals being led by the grooms of the royal stables. All of them take up their proper places on the floor of the tomb and a guard of soldiers forms up at the entrance.

'As the mournful music of the harpists sounds through the grave, each man and woman fills a little stone or metal cup he or she has brought, from a bowl of liquid in the centre of the grave bottom. This is a container of poison.

'Then everyone lies down and readies themselves for death.

'Probably the animals were then slaughtered and the earth shovelled into the hole until it was level ground once more. It's quite likely that the place was marked by the setting up of a small memorial chapel at the very top.

'It's strange to find so many human sacrifices. Although the practice isn't unknown from elsewhere, it is pretty rare.'

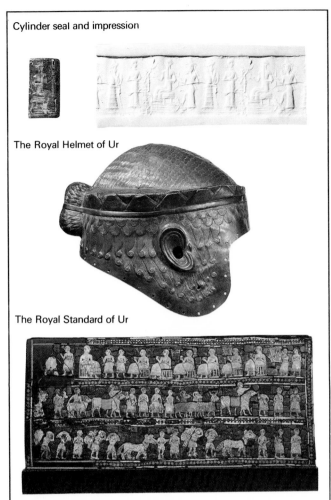

Cylinder seal and impression

The Royal Helmet of Ur

The Royal Standard of Ur

Woolley found all sorts of interesting things in other graves, for example, some beautifully fluted gold beakers, helmets, swords and daggers, necklaces and headdresses. A number of cylinder seals have also come to light but in spite of the vast number of graves, the names of only four rulers have been identified – two kings and two queens.

The body of a prince, Mes-kalam-shar was found with his head in a helmet of high quality gold. The helmet had once contained a padded cap held in place by means of a lace passed through small holes in the rim. The skull was well enough preserved to show that the prince had been left handed.

The picture above is often known as a 'royal standard' and shows the king at a civilian banquet. A second panel shows him among his soldiers on the right, accompanied by chariots with solid wheels drawn by asses. The standard is made of lapis lazuli and mother of pearl embedded in asphalt on a wooden base. Archaeologists call it a 'standard' but no one really knows what it is. However, it does give us a useful insight into the life of a king of Ur, possibly 5,000 years ago.

Section 5 *Sumer*

Babylon

The Land Of the two Rivers had been first settled in a civilised way far to the south of the region – in an area called Sumer. This had been overrun by the Akkadians, their neighbours to the north west. Then Babylon rose supreme over all other cities, particularly under Hammurabi. After his time a new power appeared – again to the northwest and up river from the Persian Gulf. This new power was based on the city of Assur.

The inhabitants of Assur are known to us as Assyrians. The Assyrians carved out an empire including Babylon. Their might lasted for centuries but had waned by about 600 B.C.

Once again Babylon became a great and powerful city. Under its kings, Nabopalassar (626–605 B.C.) and his son, the better known Nebuchadrezzar (604–561 B.C.), Babylon was to reach its greatest glory and to become for the last time, 'the mistress of the world'. The whole region came to be called 'Babylonia'.

Section 5 *Sumer*

Science in Babylon

If you grow vegetables in your garden, how do you know when to plant the seeds? 'That's easy,' you say, 'just look on the packet.' But suppose there are no packets and that the only food you are going to eat is that which you've grown yourself. It comes down to knowing when the seasons start and finish and to the exact length of the year. On p.53 we saw how ancient peoples worked out an answer to the question, 'How long is a year?'

If you live in a sunny country as they did you could put a stick in the ground and measure its shadow several times every day until you get the shortest measurement of all. This will be at twelve noon on midsummer day. Then you can count the days until the shadow is as short as that again.

The Babylonians found that their first count, although not very accurate, was a very handy number.

The figure was 360 which will divide exactly by 2, 3, 4, 5, 6, 8, 9, 10, 12, 15, 18, 20, 24, 30, 36, 40, 45, 60, 72, 90, 120 and 180. How convenient this was for anyone trying to design a calendar and what a wide choice of unit time lengths. Why do we have twelve months in the year or seven days in the week? Why 60 seconds in the minute and the same number of minutes in an hour? Why, for that matter, are there 360 degrees in a circle? No one knows the answer to these questions – all we are sure of is that the wise men of the twin valleys first decided these matters.

Of course, all this was very fine until someone spoilt things by discovering that there weren't in fact 360 days in the year. It didn't take long in Babylonia to see what was wrong: if you based your farming life on a calendar of twelve thirty-day months, you'd be five days out at the return of the next midsummer and in less than 40 years, you'd be celebrating the longest summer day on the shortest winter one!

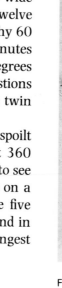

Finding noon on the shortest day

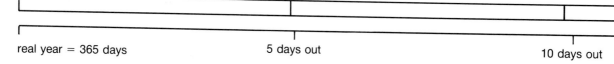

Babylonian year
Real year

(5 years Babylonian time scale) = 360 days

real year = 365 days   5 days out   10 days out

It says a great deal for the wise men that they eventually got it about right. They studied more than the movements of the earth round the sun. They also kept records of the moon's phases so carefully over many years that they were able to predict eclipses.

The fact that they were good at astronomy is even more remarkable because there were no telescopes in those days. All their observations were made with no artificial aids at all. Their best chance was to go to the top terraces of the local ziggurat and stare up at the night sky.

In this way they were able to group the stars in what to them were recognizable pictures of people, things and animals. These constellations, as they are called, formed a zodiac, or complete band round the heavens.

The wise men then attempted to predict the future from the movements of the heavenly bodies. They identified Mars, which they called Nergal, after their god of the lower world. The war god, Ninurta was what we know as Saturn. They also understood the apparent movements of Mercury, Venus and Jupiter, which were named respectively, Nabû, Ishtar and Marduk.

Science, religion and superstition went hand in hand. Observations of the stars and planets were good and accurate. Less scientific were their attempts to tell fortunes from their movement. Even more questionable, though just as popular, was the casting of horoscopes from the livers of animals.

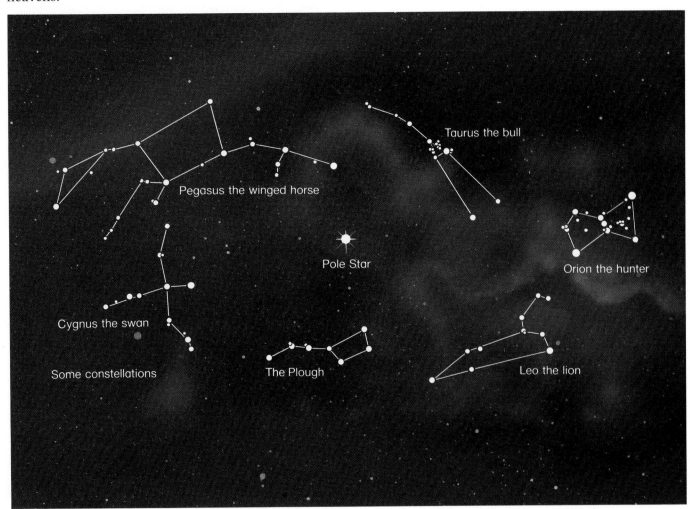

How some modern astrologers imagine the constellations

15 days out   20 days out   25 days out

Section 5 *Sumer*

Reading the wedge-shaped writing

We saw on p. 58–59 a little of how ancient Mesopotamian languages were set down in clay tablets. What we didn't find out is how people of our own time can read what was written over 5,000 years ago.

At some time in the past, the knowledge of reading and writing these ancient languages was lost. This was why, when travellers from the middle ages onward brought back stories of ruins and inscriptions from Mesopotamia, the little wedge signs were often dismissed as mere decoration. It wasn't until after 1700 that a few Europeans began to suspect that they were, in fact, some unknown language.

The men who became interested were German, English, French and Danish. Carsten Niebuhr, an engineer officer in the Danish army, copied Persian inscriptions and published them in 1765. He was the first person to decide (correctly) that they should be read from left to right and that there was more than one script involved.

Friedrich Münter, another Dane, noticed that one group of signs:

kept on turning up and he assumed it probably stood for 'king'. Georg Grotefend, a German, agreed and added another group which frequently went with the first one. This, he guessed meant 'son of'. With 'king' and 'son of the king', it became possible to say that the groups following stood for names. In this way, he managed to decipher 'Darius' and his son 'Xerxes', the names of two Persian kings, familiar to us from the pages of Greek history.

This was the only success he had and it was left to others to increase the number of signs that could be read – partly from the lists of conquered nations which also appeared in the inscriptions.

The most adventurous of the decoders was an Englishman named Henry Rawlinson. He learned Latin and Greek at school and added Arabic, Persian and Hindustani later. As an employee of the East India Company he was sent to Persia where he became very interested in the carved wedges. He was told of a large inscription some twenty miles away at Behistun.

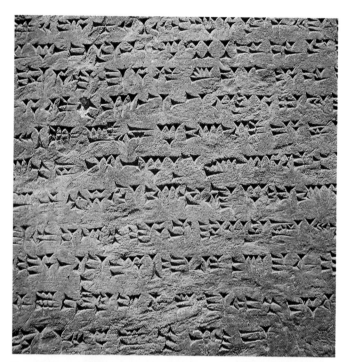

Sumerian clay tablet

Rawlinson

Unfortunately, the carvings were 300 feet up a sheer cliff. To get close, Rawlinson had to climb down a rope or be lowered in a kind of bosun's chair. He had a ladder lowered but the ledge it was to stand on was so narrow, he couldn't set it at a safe angle. Nothing daunted he climbed it and balanced on the top rung, at the same time copying the carved marks.

At one point he tried to cross to another part of the monument and the only way he could bridge the chasm was by wedging his ladder over the gap thus:

Halfway across, he suddenly felt the lower upright and half the rungs fall away from under his feet and he had to scramble back to safety, but he managed to record two of the inscriptions entirely. The third, apparently in old Babylonian, seemed to be totally out of reach. Then a young Kurdish boy volunteered to swarm upwards and sideways over a rockface which seemed to have neither foot nor fingerhold.

Now owning copies of all the writings, Rawlinson quickly made out the names of Persian kings and also some syllable signs from the names of Persia's enemies. Finally he was able to read, 'I am Darius, the great king, king of kings, king of Persia—' etc. Then follows his ancestry and an account of those of his forbears. At the end is carved, 'You who pass by in the future will see this inscription which I ordered to be made. Leave my monument as it is: destroy nothing: efface nothing. As long as Man shall last on earth, keep it intact.'

That was in old Persian but the Babylonian part was not nearly so easy. To start with, there were far too many different signs for it to be in an alphabet. The royal names could be identified and some sounds obtained but at that point (for the time being) Rawlinson could get no further. Then in 1850, the Rev. Hincks discovered that a single sign could be pronounced in perhaps half a dozen ways. Furthermore, it could stand for a word, a part of a word or even act as a pointer to show what kind of a word was coming next.

If we had the same thing in English, for example, we might draw [image] for the word 'mat', or we could use it with other signs to make words such as 'material', 'mathematics', 'automatic', which have nothing to do with the original meaning. On top of this, the sign would also appear in front of every word which belonged to the same class, for example, carpet, floor, wood blocks, concrete, lino, tiles and so on.

It made things very difficult, but gradually, the stone carvings and clay tablets gave up their secrets and we can now read most of anything written in the many languages of the Land of the Two Rivers.

Section 6 *Egypt*

Before the pyramids

Experts on ancient Egypt are known as Egyptologists. Let's ask one of them to tell us what the land was like before the pharaohs appeared on the scene.

'It's very difficult,' he begins, 'to say anything very definite – for all sorts of reasons. You see, we're talking about a period before writing was invented, so everything has to be found out from whatever the people left behind them.

'There's even a snag to digging up Egypt's long gone past. Lower or northern Egypt around the Nile Delta was where many prehistoric peoples lived. The trouble is that farming, flooding, irrigation and the buildings of later inhabitants have destroyed the traces of the earliest tribes. The only thing to do is to dig at sites a long way up the river where remains haven't been obliterated. Then we can use what we find to make guesses about the rest of the country.'

'What were those early tribes called?'

'I'm afraid I don't know. I can't see any way that we'll ever know. Remember that there was no writing then. All we can do is to label the various peoples with the names of the places where their remains were first found. For example, the Tasians from Deir Tasa, or the Badarians from El Badari.

'The various groups most likely came from outside Egypt, attracted no doubt by the rich farmlands of the valley. There are of course some even earlier peoples but of these there are only skimpy remains plus a few skeletons. Some years ago an old stone age cemetery was unearthed about 150 miles north of the Aswan dam. There were nearly sixty men, women and children and a good half of them had died by violence. but as I say we know little or nothing of their lives, which probably came to an end some 12,000 years ago. Strangely enough, we have sickles and grinders showing Man as a farmer which are at least 3,000 years older than that.

'Perhaps it was wild grain that attracted people to the valley in the first place. We know that Man reaped natural seeds long before he hit on the idea of growing them deliberately. There must have been more vegetation in those days – the valley was wetter and there were many small feeder streams. Today they are just wadis – dry water courses.

'We think that the tribes who lived there found that they could grow more food than they could eat. This led to a big increase in population and then once more there were shortages. More land had to be put under the plough. The ancient Egyptians began to drain marshes and bring life giving water to dry areas.

'The ditch could serve both purposes. In wet regions, water would seep out of the surrounding earth into the furrow. The latter could also lead water from the river to the parched fields. It could be used both for drainage and irrigation.

'At a time just before Egypt became a kingdom, the farmers had tamed the goat, sheep, pig and cow. They grew their food, raised their animals and lived in little round reed huts. They had clay pottery and from the pictures they painted on it we know what they looked like.

'They were slimly built people, of medium height with brown skins and black or dark brown wavy hair. They mostly wore kilts of animal hides, although they did sometimes weave clothing from linen thread. They could make baskets and knew how to store their extra food in mat-lined grain pits. They wore beads and bracelets made of ivory and sea shells. They even painted their eyelids with green paint – whether for beauty's sake or to protect their sight from the sun, we don't know.'

'You said something about Egypt becoming a kingdom.'

'Yes. All the extensive irrigation and drainage work meant lots of people working but not growing food. There had to be someone to run things and that's when overseers and local headmen arose. Gradually more and more small areas joined together. It must have been an advantage for the areas which combined. It's not just a question of being able to do a common task quicker or better. I'm sure you can imagine circumstances where a certain piece of work could be done by a whole population but not at all by one person. Think of dragging a hundred ton stone to strengthen a river bank, for example.

'Anyway, the process went on and on, until about 3,200 B.C., the whole valley, both Upper and Lower Egypt, was united by a man called variously Narmer, or Menes. He was the first pharaoh.'

Menes (Narmer) palette from Hierakonpolis

Pre-pyramid Egyptian village

The discovery of metal

At the time when Menes was becoming the first pharaoh of the first dynasty, or family, many Egyptians were still using stone tools and implements. Many, but not all. For some time before this, unknown people had discovered the first metal.

This was copper. There were at that time places where lumps of it could be picked up. You may imagine a stone age man trying to strike flakes off it as he could do with a nodule of flint. The copper merely took a dent. It wasn't long before Man learnt how to hammer out his copper lump to form rings, pins and bracelets. Then he discovered the art of making edged tools such as axes, knives and daggers.

These discoveries were not necessarily made in Egypt at all and in any case there wasn't a great deal of metallic copper lying about, so it was a lucky day when someone hit on a method of making metal from a copper ore. This is copper combined with some other mineral, for example, oxygen, sulphur or carbon.

The coppersmith had to heat lumps of the ore in heat-resistant pots over an extremely hot fire. An ordinary bonfire isn't really hot enough so a charcoal oven was probably used and its temperature raised with bellows. If you can shoot a jet of fresh oxygen-laden air into your fire, it glows brighter and reaches a higher temperature.

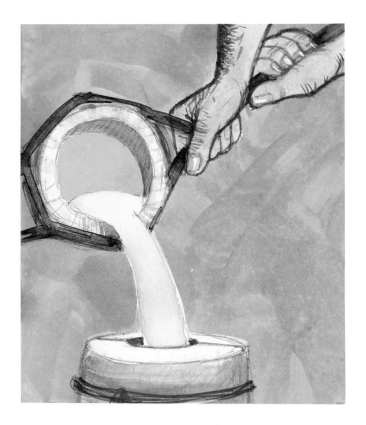

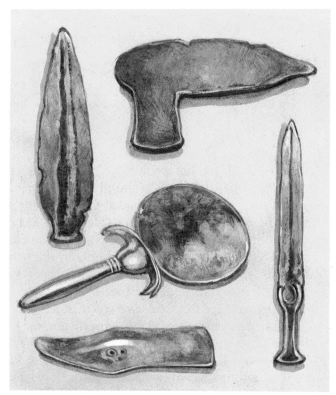

Early bronze objects

The Egyptians used a kind of foot bellows, consisting of a pair of animal-skin bags whose mouths led into pottery funnels. These conducted air to the fire. The smith's assistant stood with a foot on each bag. There might be as many as four helpers doing the same thing. A helper lifted one foot and at the same time pulled up the middle of the bag with a leather thong. Then he pushed his foot down to blow air into the tube, at the same time lifting his other leg – a sort of marking time.

The copper ore in the pot melted and the metal could be poured out like a liquid. The smith then treated the solidified puddle in the same way as he dealt with natural metal lumps.

Then someone thought it would save time if the molten metal could be poured straight into a shape, made perhaps from stone or clay. A lump of limestone with hollows scraped out could produce, say, several knife blades at one melting. From there it was a short step to an upright mould with its top end open. This could be used for a variety of more complicated shapes.

The search for copper ores went on. As soon as they were found, methods discovered from flint mining were put into operation. More often than not, the ores were not pure, having various minerals mixed with them – tin, antimony or arsenic were among these impurities. When they were present and became part of the smelting process, a new metal was produced. We call it bronze.

It was a little harder than copper or tin on their own but it flowed more easily into the moulds. The bronze-smith, as we must now call him, began to mix the two ores deliberately, altering the amounts of each that were used until he got the metal he wanted. There was very little tin in Egypt, so it either had to be bought abroad, or the Egyptians had to do without, using arsenic instead.

One metal that was plentiful in Egypt was gold. Prospectors panned for it in river gravels and eventually it was dug from underground mines.

Surprisingly, iron was also known in the Nile valley – and from a time almost as early as copper, bronze or gold. It wasn't mined though – it occurred as lumps of meteorite which had crashed from outer space and there wasn't much of it.

One trouble was that although copper melts at just over 1,000° centigrade, iron won't do so until it's half as hot again. Early Man couldn't produce temperatures like these and it wasn't in fact until the later middle ages that furnaces were made to generate so much heat.

All the Eygptian craftsman could do if he got the rare chance to work on a chunk of heavenly iron was to heat it as much as possible and then hammer out the impurities. Amid showers of sparks, repeated blows gradually turned the iron ore into a metal. Bronze remained the most important metal for the next two thousand years.

Building temples and pyramids

If there is one thing that seems like a trade mark to the modern Egyptian tourist it is the pyramid. Pyramids have filled travellers with wonder from the earliest times. They seem such a colossal waste of time, energy and wealth. Where did the riches to pay for them come from? We've already seen how peasants in the valley could easily grow three times as much food as they needed. The surplus could be traded abroad for the things Egypt lacked but there was still a lot left over. it was this extra wealth that fed the armies of non-farmers who were used to carry out all kinds of grand schemes.

Menes and the pharaohs who followed him were able to spend this wealth as they wished. However, it was four centuries after the reign of Menes before the first pyramid was built.

For many years the cult of the dead had been growing. Egyptians firmly believed in an after life, particularly for their dead king who was expected to plead to the gods for the well-being of his people. Gods, naturally, they thought, would pay little heed to a man with few possessions and would only deal with some-one of their own social class. So the custom arose of burying the dead ruler with all his favourite treasures.

In earlier times, the dead (even common people) were buried in the ground; sometimes flat stones were set around the body and on top of it to prevent it being dug up by wild animals. This developed into a low rectangular stone building called a mastaba.

These got larger and more elaborate as the years went by until in the reign of the pharaoh Djoser (about 2750 B.C.) the first pyramid was built. It was designed as the king's tomb by one of ancient Egypt's most outstanding men, the minister of state, Imhotep.

Imhotep, had many talents: as well as being in charge of the court's religion, he was also an author, a wise man, an astronomer, a doctor and above all, a very great architect.

It may not be so, but it seems as though Imhotep had laid out an enormous mastaba and had then placed a slightly smaller one on top. He was to do this a further three times, finally winding up with a wonder of the age, over 200 feet high. Inside the pyramid was a maze of corridors joining rooms and the whole building was surrounded by a wall about ten metres high and almost two kilometres long.

Djoser

Imhotep

A step pyramid

The pyramid of Cheops

From then on, most pharaohs and many other important persons had pyramids built to house their dead bodies and as rich a selection of precious goods as could be afforded. Probably the most important pyramid was that of the pharaoh Cheops. It was built about 2650 B.C. and is the largest of all – in fact, almost certainly the biggest single building in the world, if one excepts the Great Wall of China.

Its size is really remarkable. Each of its four sides measures 750 feet and its height is a mighty 474 feet. Do you know what this is?

Yes, you've guessed – it's a map showing 8 football pitches side by side. This huge area would be only just large enough to take the base of the Great Pyramid.

The stone with which this enormous tomb is constructed was quarried on the spot but the shining white limestone cladding was ferried across the river. All told, more than two million blocks were cut and moved. The largest stones weighed about 15 tonnes, although the average was only two tonnes. If you were to cut up each stone into rods three inches square and put them end to end, there would be enough of them to reach from the earth to the moon!

No one knows what kinds nor how many men worked on the Great Pyramid. In ancient times, Greek visitors were told that it had taken 100,000 slaves ten years but this is probably an exaggeration – it's likely that there were few slaves among the work force.

Another mystery is the method they used to haul the massive stones into position. We think that they were split in the quarry, roughly squared and then pulled away on sledges or wooden rollers.

The first layer was positioned from the centre outwards until the marked out square was full, making allowance of course for all the galleries, stairs, passages and tomb chambers. Then a ramp of stones, clay, mud bricks and sand was led to the top of the first course of blocks, up which the stones for the second course were hauled. As each layer was put in place, the ramp was lengthened and made higher. Some authorities say that the ramp may have wound round the half finished building. The last few stones were set in position and the outer skin of dazzling white limestone was added.

Some of Egypt's most striking temples were also built with the aid of ramps. An oblong of bedrock was cleared and levelled before the position of the columns was marked. These were prefabricated in drum-shaped pieces. The first drums were manoeuvered into line and the spaces between and all round them filled in with hard-packed sand and dirt. Then ramps were made and the next layer of stone column drums moved in. When the pillars were complete they were joined at the top with spans of roofing stone. When all was over, the packing earth and ramps were dug away.

The inside of a pyramid, showing internal passages, staircases and burial room

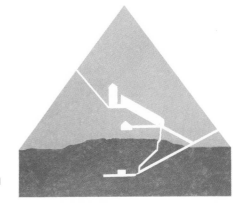

The oldest ship in the world

Have you ever noticed the rather pleasant smell that comes from a newly sharpened pencil? If you have, the pencil was probably made from a cedar tree. How long do you think the wood might go on pouring out this scent – a week, a month, a year? Kamal el-Mallakh from the Egyptian Antiquities Service could still detect the special cedar smell from timber which had been buried for forty-five centuries.

How did this come about? Shortly after the end of the Second World War, the Egyptian government decided to tidy up some of the pyramids near Cairo.

At Giza, just across the Nile from Egypt's capital, stands a group of pyramids among which is that of Cheops, the largest of them all. Archaeologists working on nearby tombs had dumped unwanted soil at the base of the Great Pyramid.

The workmen slowly cleared the dirt and sand from the north, east and west sides without finding anything exciting. Then they began to shift the spoil from the south side. Although the heap was 65 feet high, they couldn't just bulldoze it away for fear of destroying something of interest.

However, nothing turned up and they finally came to a line of smooth limestone slabs almost 15 feet wide and nearly two feet thick. One stone stood up slightly higher than the others and Mallakh recognised the hieroglyphic: It read 'Djedefre'. He knew that this king was the son of Cheops and suspected that these stones might cover a boat pit. Several of these were already known but all that had ever been found in them were a few scraps of wood and some decayed strands of rope to show that there had once been a vessel buried there.

At about midday on the 26th May 1954, the workmen managed to finish chipping a hole through the stones. The sun was so hot and bright that Mallakh could see nothing but blackness, so he used a small mirror to reflect sunlight into the pit and peered down. Was it a boat? He held his breath. The beam caught and held the sight he had hardly dared hope for – the blade of a long rowing oar. It was then that Mallakh became aware of the faint but unmistakable sent of cedar wood.

A piece of the planking was taken to the British Museum chemical laboratories and proved to be not

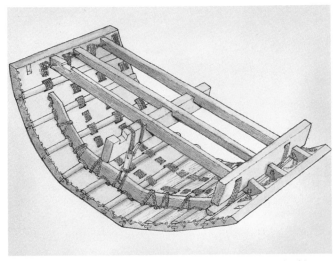

How the planks were joined together, by being lashed (or sewn) with rope

The burial ship in pieces, as it was found

only cedar wood of the right age but surprisingly well preserved. The sealing of the pit with stones and wet mortar had prevented the timber from drying out and turning to dust.

A shed was built over the boat grave and the stones removed by cranes. This took two months.

Hadj Ahmed Youssef Moustafa, in charge of the restoration, faced many problems. The ship was in pieces and had to be assembled like a 3D jigsaw puzzle. Each piece had to be drawn and photographed before it was moved and treated with chemicals to prevent decay. There was, of course, no picture or instruction booklet to help him, so Moustafa had scale models made of each piece – all 1224 of them. The planking turned out to be 'sewn' together with rope, of which there were great lengths. The rope went into a hole on the wide part of the plank and out through the edge, so that no rope could be seen on the outside.

A special museum was built on the site and Moustafa made five different reconstructions before he was satisfied. The finished vessel is over 142 feet long, nearly 20 feet across as its widest part and would displace about 45 tonnes. From beginning to end, the project took fourteen years.

The royal ship of Cheops was probably used to take his body from Memphis to Giza. Although there were five pairs of oars between 20 and 30 feet long, it is quite likely that the vessel was towed down the River Nile before being taken to pieces and buried.

It remains to this day the oldest, largest and best preserved vessel from the ancient world.

Section 6 *Egypt*

Cleopatra's needle

Most people have seen or at least heard of Cleopatra's needle on London's Victoria Embankment, alongside the River Thames. The word 'needle' may give you the wrong idea if you've never even seen a photograph of it. Another word is 'obelisk' and this means a tall column whose four sides gradually taper to the top where a small pyramid finishes it off. The Egyptians put up many of these columns – as signs, memorials or monuments.

If 'needle' is not too happy a word, then 'Cleopatra' is even more ill-chosen. The Thameside column has little, if anything, to do with the famous queen. It was, in fact, erected on the orders of Thotmes III* many centuries before Cleopatra's time. Originally at Heliopolis, it was moved to Alexandria during the reign of the Roman emperor, Augustus. The move occurred at about 12 B.C., when the obelisk was already almost fifteen centuries old.

Cleopatra's needle, London

In 1819 A.D., the Viceroy of Egypt presented the thing to the British people. A special vessel to contain it was built. After a series of misfortunes, including its near loss crossing the Bay of Biscay in a storm, it finally arrived on the Thames. It was not set up in its present position until 1878. Under the base, the Victorians buried a British railway timetable, a copy of *The Times* and some current coins.

The 'needle' is covered with carved Egyptian writing as are the other obelisks in Rome, Paris, Istanbul and New York. The American one is the twin of ours but the others are from different places and of different ages. The Romans began the custom by taking several obelisks back home with them – just like tourists collecting souvenirs. Of course, they had the same problem as the original owners whenever they wanted to set one up again. At least the Victorian British had steam engines to help them – but how did the Pharaoh's men manage? Let's ask one.

'I wouldn't say it was easy but there aren't any really unsolvable problems. To start with, you need very many people to help – sometimes only a handful of men, sometimes thousands.

*Thotmes is only one of several English versions of the name: others include: Thotmose, Thothmes, Tutmose, Tuthmosis, Tutmoss, etc.

'Only the best stone will do. We get much of ours from Syene. It is a hard, pink granite. We make sure that the piece we are going to work on is free from flaws or cracks. We wash it down thoroughly and then inspect it. It's easier to break out if it's on the edge of a low lip of rock in the quarry. The shape is outlined with paint made of animal fat and ground charcoal. Then metal chisels make holes along a line. When the holes are deep enough, large wooden wedges are driven in and surrounded by low clay walls. Water is poured in, the wood swells and, if we are lucky, the stone splits along the line we want and we can topple it sideways onto rollers. It's much harder if we have to dig all the way down through solid granite with chisels and stone hammers – a long and tiring job.

'At last the obelisk is free and ready to be worked on. The stone masons can get it smooth and polish the sides until they shine but it needs the special skills of the scribe/stone carver to add the writing. The finishing touch is the capping of the top pyramid part with metal, often gold.

'With levers, rollers, ropes and thousands of workers, we slowly move the huge mass down to the water's edge. It's far easier, when you've got to move a thing this size, to use a boat.

'When we get to journey's end we have to unload by doing in reverse what we did to load up at the quarry. Then we manoeuvre the obelisk to its final position. It's quite tricky getting it to stand up. Gangs of men are ordered to make a hill with a height just over half that of the pillar. It has to have a steep slope one side, opposite a gentle gradient.

'Then with hundreds of men on ropes, levers and rollers, we nudge the thing up the slope and hope we've worked it out so accurately that the obelisk tips up onto its base and stands upright in the right place.'

We thank him and think about the muscle power needed to shift these enormous masses of stone. The smaller of the obelisks were not much higher than a tall man but some of the larger ones were so big, it's hard to imagine them being moved at all. Perhaps the biggest are to be found, not standing proudly erect but sill in the quarry where they were left thousands of years ago. Although an average height might be about 70 feet, the one still lying at Aswan weighs well over a thousand tonnes.

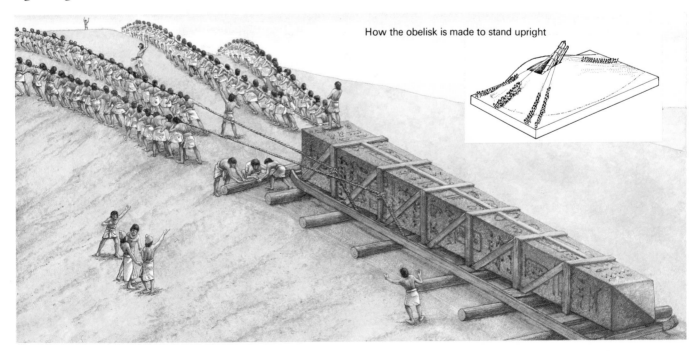

How the obelisk is made to stand upright

Section 6 *Egypt*

Mummies and tombs

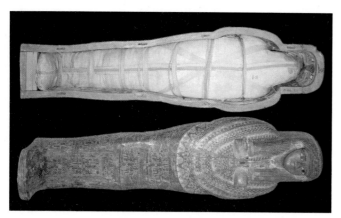

A mummy

Perhaps we could ask our Egyptologist about this. 'What is a mummy?' we say.

He laughs. 'It's not a children's word for mother,' he says, 'It's actually an Arabic word meaning 'wax'. Arabs were the first people in modern times to find the preserved dead bodies of ancient Egyptians. Some of the earliest had been crudely dipped in pitch. The first Egyptians believed that you couldn't go to heaven if you didn't have a body to go in. They also thought that each one of them had a spirit 'double', or 'ka'. After death the ka could leave the corpse and consume the food and drink left for it in the tomb. But should the body be destroyed, then that was the end of the ka and the end of immortality.

Papyrus picture of 'Ka' from the *Egyptian Book of the Dead*

'We think that the idea of deliberately trying to preserve the dead body occurred to the people after it had happened accidentally. In the British Museum is the corpse of a peasant who died and was found over 5,000 years later in good condition, thanks to the hot sand which had blown across and covered it.

The preserved Egyptian peasant from the British Museum

'At the time of the first pharaohs, priests tried at least to keep the shape of the corpse by binding the trunk, head, limbs (even the separate fingers) with gum-soaked bandages. When the gum dried the linen strips still showed the outline of the body no matter what had happened to the flesh inside.

'Eventually the priests worked out the best ways of embalming. The dead person was brought to them and they began by removing the inner organs. To put it crudely, it was a bit like gutting a fish before smoking or drying it! Except for the heart, the organs were put in canopic jars. These were made of pottery and usually had a sculptured human head on top. The brain was hooked out by way of the nostrils and the body was then ready for the treatment. It was laid in a wooden box and covered with natron crystals.'

'What's natron?'

'A chemical often found at the edges of lakes. Its proper name is hydrated carbonate of soda and it can soak up 75% of the water a human body is composed of. The process took ten weeks, at the end of which the shrinking was practically complete.

'The skull was packed with natron and plaster, then artificial eyes of black stone were set in place. The heart

very wealthy family, such as that of a pharaoh, would provide the costliest funeral of all with an outer stone container, or sarcophagus.

'A pharaoh's body, bound for burial in a pyramid was probably carried along the Nile on a specially built boat and delivered to the outbuildings for the embalming. It was then taken along a covered causeway to the building where almost the last ceremonies were held. Eventually the bearers moved the royal coffin to its final resting place in the heart of the pyramid.'

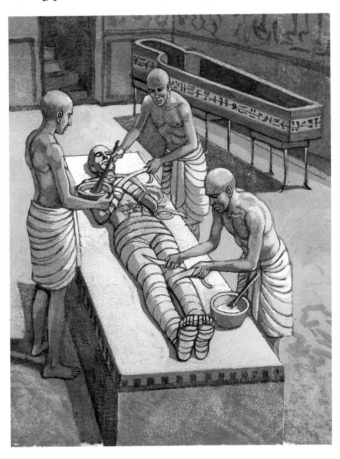

was put back and held in position with wads of linen rags. At each stage the priests chanted prayers and spells and added lucky charms to the corpse. The wealthier the dead person, the richer were the jewels laid on the body which was ready for bandaging after being rubbed with ointments.

'The linen strips were soaked in a solution of natron and the swathing began. Occasionally, a prayer for the dead written on papyrus paper would be bound in. Sometimes the prayer was inked straight onto the linen. These were supposed to ward off evil spirits.

'Only the very rich could afford all the rites and processes in the early days but gradually things became cheaper and thus more common. A poor person's funeral might make use of a nearly plain wooden box for the corpse with just a line or two of prayer painted on the lid. Those who could afford better would have several coffins, one inside the other, each elaborately painted with sacred verses, the name of the departed and representations of the various gods. Now and then, an imaginary map of the land of the dead was painted on the bottom of the coffin. The inner coffin was shaped roughly to the same outline as the finished mummy. A

The Egyptologist sighs but goes on. 'Unfortunately, all the pyramids were robbed of their precious contents within a very few years of the burial. The tomb builders did all in their power to fool the thieves. They made false doors, staircases and corridors. They would put a blocking stone at the end of a passageway and plaster it in. The idea was that the thieves would break through only to find solid rock behind, whilst the real way forward was via a trapdoor in the ceiling.

'As I say, every pyramid and all but two of the rock tombs were stripped of their treasures.'

We thank him and move off. The two rock tombs we later learn are those of Tutankhamen and Queen Hetepheres, the mother of Cheops, builder of the Great Pyramid. We'll find out later how they were found.

Akhenaten and religion

Osiris

We see a family coming from a temple, dedicated to the god Osiris. We ask the father about religion.

'We Egyptians are very religious,' he says, 'We believe in many gods and goddesses and make magic a part of our everyday lives.'

'Magic?' we ask, disbelievingly.

'Certainly,' he says, 'all the religions I know have magic in them or superstition, I suppose you might call it – you know, things that defy logic. Take this story of Osiris, one of our greatest gods.

'He started as a simple earth god. He is credited with inventing farming and wine making. The shepherd's crook and the farmer's corn flail, carried by all pharaohs, are his signs. In this story, his brother Seth was jealous of him and persuaded him by a trick to step into a wooden box. Seth shut the lid and locked it, then threw the chest into the Nile, where Osiris drowned. The magic is that he came back to life. In fact, another version of the story has Osiris's body being hacked to pieces and his wife finding the parts in different regions of Egypt and sewing them together again. We think the drowning and coming-to-life story really stands for the life-giving Nile floods which make the growing of crops possible.'

'But the two stories can't both be true.'

'Why not? It's quite possible for us to believe things that disagree with each other. For example, we have a goddess with two names – Bastet and Sekhmet. Bastet is a friendly cat which the women like to make a fuss of. But under her second name she has the head of a lioness on a human body and is shown as a lover of killing, slaughter, butchery and cannibalism.'

'Hmm, yes. What about an after life?'

'Do you know about mummies?' We nod and he goes on. 'Well, after he has passed on, the dead soul is shown into the hall of judgment by the jackal-headed god, Anubis. His heart is weighed in the scales against the feather of truth, whilst the ibis-headed god, Thoth writes down the verdict. A demon, called the 'heart-eater', who is a cross between lion, hippopotamus and crocodile, waits eagerly to be fed if there is a guilty verdict. While the weighing is going on, the dead soul

Anubis and the weighing of the soul

has to deny committing all kinds of lifetime crimes before the 42 gods on the jury. If they say 'not guilty', he is led by Horus to Osiris, the latter's father. Osiris sits on a throne in a pavilion at one end of the hall, attended by his wife, Isis and her sister, Nephthys. It is here the soul is told the verdict. The reward for his innocence is everlasting life.'

'This is for the pharaoh only?'

'It used to be but nowadays everyone wants to go to heaven so even quite poor people put food and drink in the tomb for the loved one's journey to the west. If you can afford a proper coffin in a tomb we paint a door on the side of the coffin, so that your soul can get to the food.'

'If a painted door will do instead of a real one, why bother with embalming a dead body? Can't you just pretend it isn't rotting?'

Our friend smiles and shrugs. 'There are too many gods to please,' he says, 'I've mentioned some of them but there are hundreds more. Once, not so long ago, there was a pharaoh who tried to change all that. He was annoyed that the priests of the different temples seemed to be getting more wealthy and powerful than the king.'

'Who was this ruler?'

'Amenophis. He came to the throne when his elder brother died young. His father had the same name, the third pharaoh to be so called. For a while he was known as Amenophis IV but after five or six years he changed his name to Akhenaten. He forbade the worship of all gods other than Aten, the sole god and embodiment of the golden sun. He built himself a new capital city and allowed artists to produce natural works of art. From then on, they could show people as they were and not as tradition said they should be shown. One example is this bust of Nefertiti, Akhenaten's beautiful wife.

'He ordered the closing of all "non Aten" temples and the chiselling off the names of other gods from carved inscriptions. So busy was he with these matters that he ignored military dangers and managed to lose most of the empire beyond our borders. I suppose he was intelligent – he had an enormous head but he was a most odd-looking fellow.

'There was much discontent here at home – his religious ideas never caught on with the common people. After he died, his half brother ruled for a few months but then Akhenaten's son-in-law came to the throne. He was only nine years old and had been known as Tut-ankh-aten in his father-in-law's time. He had to change his name to Tutankhamen. He died when he was only eighteen. He isn't very important and I don't suppose you've ever heard of him.'

Ahkenaten

Nefertiti

Tutankhamen's tomb

We've seen how the pyramid developed from the mastaba, but pyramids fell out of fashion because they were so easy to rob. The next development was the tomb cut into the rocky cliffs lining the Valley of the Kings. In spite of this, no one in modern times has ever found a royal grave completely untouched and un-robbed. As we can now account for most of ancient Egyptian royal burials, the chances are that we never will. The nearest we ever came to finding one was in the case of Tutankhamen. We ought to ask the Egyptologist who actually found the tomb to tell us about it.

'My name is Howard Carter,' he says, 'I was employed by Lord Carnarvon to look for any new tombs we might find in the Valley of the Kings. The silly thing is that a man named Ayrton, who was here before me, actually turned up some old vases marked with Tutankhamen's name. He didn't think much of them and sent them to New York's Metropolitan Museum where they were put away and forgotten. If only someone had told us of the discovery, we wouldn't have spent so long looking in the wrong place.

'In 1922, after many years of digging, my employer told me that this was to be the last year he could afford in Egypt. We went back to a little triangle of land where there were the remains of some very ancient workmen's huts. We knocked them down and found underneath many tons of rubble from the tomb of Rameses VI in the cliff above. It seemed unlikely that anything was there but the area had to be searched.

'On the morning of November 4th, I was struck by the silence. Usually the workmen were constantly chatting, laughing, shouting – now, there was nothing. I went to where the first trench was being cut: a workman's spade had struck rock. It proved to be the top step of a stone staircase going down into the rock. It took us three days to uncover as far as the twelfth step. When we did I saw the plastered up top of a possible doorway. I was sure we were on to something import-ant. There was a seal on the doorway from the ancient Royal Cemetery Commission but nothing to tell us whose last resting place it was.

The first view inside the tomb

Entering the sealed chamber

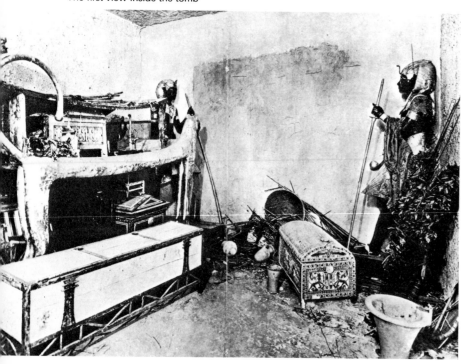

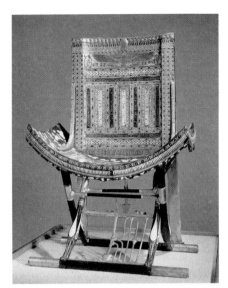

Objects found in Tutankhamen's tomb

'I had the steps filled in again and sent a telegram to his lordship, telling him what had happened. He got here in only eighteen days and we opened up the staircase once more – right down to the bottom of the door. A seal of Tutankhamen was found – but worryingly, it showed signs of having been fixed more than once. I thought to myself, 'Have the thieves beaten us to it once again?'

'I made a hole in the door but all I could see was rubble. We removed the door and the rubbish behind it and found a second door along a short passageway. Again there were signs of breaking and resealing. My heart sank.

'I made a hole in the top left hand corner of the door and put a candle into the gap. A gust of hot, dry air from inside made the flame flicker. Then the guttering stopped, the flame steadied and I could see inside. What met my gaze was a room full of things – couches, chariot wheels, boxes, animal models, jumbled furniture, chests – and everywhere the glint of gold.

'Very carefully we removed the door and began to check on what we'd found. There were so many things to draw, photograph and measure, that it was three months before we'd cleared the room. It was obvious that although thieves had been in the antechamber and had forced open some of the caskets, they must have been interrupted, for the contents had been hastily bundled back again. There didn't seem to be anything missing.

'We removed a third doorway – the one to the burial chamber – on February 17th 1923. A wall of gold was revealed. It was part of a gilt wooden screen. There were four of these shrines, one inside the other, surrounding an enormous sandstone sarcophagus. Inside was a nest of three coffins – two of gilded wood and one of gold.

Within the last lay the king's mummy with a gold face mask and gold protectors for the fingers and toes. Scattered about the corpse and covered by the linen bandages were dozens of jewels and lucky charms.

'There were two other small rooms to investigate and a tremendous number of items to list, including a chariot, couches inlaid with gold and ivory, chairs, tables, storage chests, games, clothing, gloves, a throne with the young ruler and his queen pictured on the back rest. Many of the caskets were ornamented with hunting or battle scenes.

'The whole effect was overwhelming and made huge newspaper headlines all over the world. Any one object would have been reward enough for a year's digging.

'One thought keeps coming back to me. If they could bury this unimportant king with so much splendour (and in haste, too) whatever must the tomb of a well established pharaoh have looked like? Unfortunately, we'll never know – all the tombs were robbed – and in the lifetime of those mourners who were at the funeral. What a pity!'

Tutankhamen's death mask

Tutankhamen's scarab and scarab bracelet

Section 6 *Egypt*

The lost toy cupboard

In March 1920, an Egyptologist decided to make a plan of a previously explored tomb west of Thebes. He had cleared out most of the rubble, when a workman drew his attention to a crack in the floor down which some of the swept up dust was disappearing. Puzzled, he had the stone removed and found himself gazing down into yet another tomb.

It hadn't belonged to a famous pharaoh but to a royal civil servant named Meketre. What made it interesting were the wooden models which the room contained. It was as if a child had put his toys away for the last time and never returned to play with them again. This toy cupboard, however, had been closed and forgotten for 4,000 years!

In reality, these were models intended to assist the departed soul in heaven – but they have given us a marvellous picture of the life style enjoyed by a wealthy man who lived a time that was farther in the past to Jesus Christ than He is to us today.

These are not great works of art and they have no hieroglyphic inscriptions accompanying them, yet they tell us a great deal about upper class daily life in ancient Egypt.

Yacht

House and garden

Brewery and bakery

Everyday life

We've seen how farming was done in the great river valleys, including that of the Nile. More than 90% of the population spent most of their time farming. Wheat for bread and barley for beer have been mentioned but many other things were grown.

Among the vegetables produced were onions, radishes, peas and beans, leeks, garlic, cucumbers and lettuces. In his orchard, the well-to-do Egyptian might grow gourds, melons, figs, dates and grapes. The last two, as well as being fruits, were also used to make wine.

Although donkeys and cows worked on Egyptian farms, they also (together with ewes) gave milk, both for drinking and making into cheese. Sheep provided wool and both they and the cows and bulls were butchered for their meat. Poor farmers tended to keep goats rather than cattle or sheep and they and their families sometimes ate pork although the priests said that pig meat was forbidden, as it was an unclean animal.

Other sources of meat were geese, ducks, cranes and wild waterfowl. The eggs of these birds were eagerly looked for as well. Rich people, such as the pharaoh and his courtiers might enjoy the flesh of gazelles or antelopes which they had hunted and killed in the dried up watercourses on the fringes of the desert.

Like pork, certain kinds of fish were held to be sacred in some places but this didn't stop peasants adding them to a diet that might have been rather monotonous otherwise.

Other things were grown that were not mostly (or not at all) intended for food, for example, flax for linen or linseed oil. Oils were also extracted from olives and from the castor oil plant. They were used as a fuel for lighting lamps or even as suntan oils!

In a tomb belonging to an upper class lady of second dynasty times, an actual meal was laid out on plates for the departed to feed on. Even after several thousand years it was still possible to identify the items on the menu. These included fish, pigeon stew, kidneys, quail, barley porridge, ribs of beef, bread rolls, small round cakes, some cherry-like fruit, plus stewed figs and finishing with cheese, wine and beer. Not the sort of thing enjoyed by peasants but a typical spread at a well-to-do dinner party.

The giver of such a feast, in common with most Egyptians, washes completely, morning and evening. He sits on a stool in a stone floored bathroom and cleans himself with soda, after which a servant pours water over him. He oils his skin and dabs on perfume. He shaves with a bronze razor, then wraps a linen kilt around his middle and slips on his sandals. Then he pulls on his wig and he is ready. Many people wear wigs, some because they are going grey or bald, others because it's the fashion. One of his bald friends has been advised to rub the top of his head with an ointment made from the fat of snakes, hippos and crocodiles.

Poor peasants couldn't afford an elaborate toilet and had to be content with a bucket of water outside the door if they wanted a bath. Young children wore few, if any clothes, so they could swim and bathe whenever they wanted, merely by diving in the nearest pond.

Beauty aids for the Egyptian woman included green and black eye paint, haematite powder or red ochre for lips and cheeks, perfume and pots of face cream. She did her hair with a bone or ivory comb and held her tresses in place with pins of the same materials. She wore a long sheath dress which went under her arms and just about reached down to her ankles. Spinners of linen yarn managed to get it so fine that the finished cloth was more like silk and almost transparent.

Jewellery of all kinds was worn by men and women. There were necklaces, anklets and bangles of ivory, copper or gold and rings set with semi-precious stones. Lucky charms such as the scarab beetle in precious metal were also worn. Both sexes were fond of elaborately jewelled necklets and all kinds of beads, particularly those of blue lapis lazuli.

Poor peasants no longer lived in reed lean-tos but in huts of mud brick. These were small and rectangular with flat roofs. In cold weather, the peasant slept under a blanket but if it was hot he tended to stretch out on the roof to catch whatever cool breezes there were. In one room the housewife ground the grain into flour which she then turned into dough and baked her bread in a clay oven in one corner. For fuel, she burned straw, the dried roots of papyrus plants, date stone charcoal, or even animal droppings.

The houses of rich people were more elaborate, even though still made of sun-dried mud bricks: only temples, tombs and monuments were completed in stone. For this reason, very few houses survive, although tomb paintings and models give us some idea of what they were like.

A typical rich man's dwelling was enclosed within a high wall. Also enclosed was a tree shaded pool surrounded by flowers and ornamental bushes. The house itself might be two stories high with the rooms opening into a central courtyard. The walls were plastered and painted. The ceiling was held up by brightly coloured wooden pillars, shaped to look like large bundles of reeds.

There was very little furniture. People sat on the mat-strewn floor or on cushions scattered along a mud brick ledge. There were a few chests and boxes in which to keep clothes and valuables and that was all, apart from some small, low, round tables which were big enough only for one or two diners each. The tables could also be used for board games – a bit like ludo or draughts. There were no dice but they did have 'dice sticks' which could be thrown to give random numbers.

The disappearing queen

In 1925 at Giza, near the Great Pyramid, a photographer who was working for an American group was just setting up his tripod when he noticed a discoloured patch of stone near his feet. The deputy director of the group ordered the men to dig it up.

Below was a staircase in the rock, rather like the one leading to Tutankhamen's tomb. This one, however, led to a deep, vertical shaft filled with blocks of limestone. The workmen began to lift them out. At a depth of thirty feet there was no sign of anything interesting. Then suddenly, a niche in the side of shaft came to light. It contained some beer jars and the remains of beef joints – all that was left of some ancient sacrifice. From then on they found more and more fragments of pottery.

When they had gone down eighty feet, they reached a double layer of carefully laid stones, which they took away, revealing the edge of a ceiling over a rock-cut room. By now it was late afternoon and the light was fading. One of the wall blocks was removed and the archaeologists could just make out the vague outlines of a stone coffin and the occasional glint of gold.

The following morning they fixed up an ingenious arrangement of mirrors, so that a ray of sunlight could be shone down into the grave.

On one side of the room stood a coffin of alabaster. Across it and all over the floor there was a tremendous jumble of bits of gold, broken pottery and masses of pieces that couldn't be identified immediately. There was scarcely room to stand in the narrow room without doing damage.

Each piece within reach had to be measured, drawn and photographed before being fitted onto a master plan. The room took two years to clear, fragment by fragment. As soon as the first scraps reached the top of the shaft, a team on the surface began to try and put together the pieces of a giant 3D jigsaw. It was extremely difficult for they had little idea of what the finished articles would look like. As they went on it became obvious from the hieroglyphic inscriptions that this was a royal tomb of Hetepheres, wife of the pharaoh Sneferu and mother of Cheops, builder of the Great Pyramid.

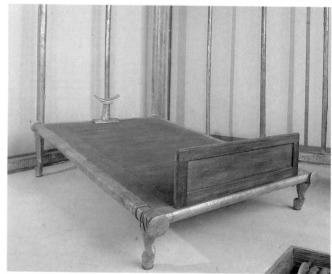

Objects found at Giza

So well was the rescue work done that the team was able to say what sizes and shapes the pieces of wood had once been from the remaining gold sheathings and inlays. When they had finished reconstructing, the items of furniture were shown to have been: one bed in ebony and sheathed in gold (beaten gold glued to a coating of plaster) with an ebony footboard inlaid with faience and carnelian. For a pillow there was a decorated ebony head rest. There was a box containing bracelets and trinkets and a chest for holding canopy curtains. Others held gold vessels and gold toilet accessories. There was a carrying chair and two armchairs. Above all, there was, when all the pieces had been fitted together, a huge, gold-covered wooden framework over which went the curtains designed to screen the furniture.

What the archaeologists couldn't understand was why the queen had been buried so secretly and in less than royal splendour, considering that she was a pharaoh's wife. They soon had another question to answer, for when the coffin was opened, it was found (apart from some stains) to be totally empty. Where was the body? Why were there all the trappings of a royal funeral if there were no corpse? What had happened?

Then another discovery was made. Inside a sealed recess in the wall they found a container with four compartments, in which were the internal organs of the queen. These, by the way, were the earliest surviving evidence of the practice of embalming. So, Hetepheres had been in the coffin once. But why was it now empty?

After a good deal of thought, the excavators themselves put forward a theory. Of course, it could never be proved but it seemed to fit the facts.

Hetepheres as the wife of Sneferu had probably been buried royally and properly near her husband's pyramid, some miles away. When her son Cheops was on the throne, robbers had broken into her grave, taken the mummy outside to remove all the gold and jewellery hidden under the linen bandages. Leaving the body to be scavenged by desert jackals, the thieves were on their way back to continue plundering the tomb when they were disturbed. They either fled or were arrested.

The officials dared not tell the pharaoh the whole story but got his permission (on some pretext or other) to rebury the grave furniture and coffin at a better protected site near the Great Pyramid, hoping that he'd never find out that his mother's body was missing. They would have breathed easier if they'd known it was to be 4,500 years before the theft was discovered. They'd also have been more than surprised to learn that even after that enormous length of time there was still some embalming fluid left in the canopic container!

Grave robbers at work

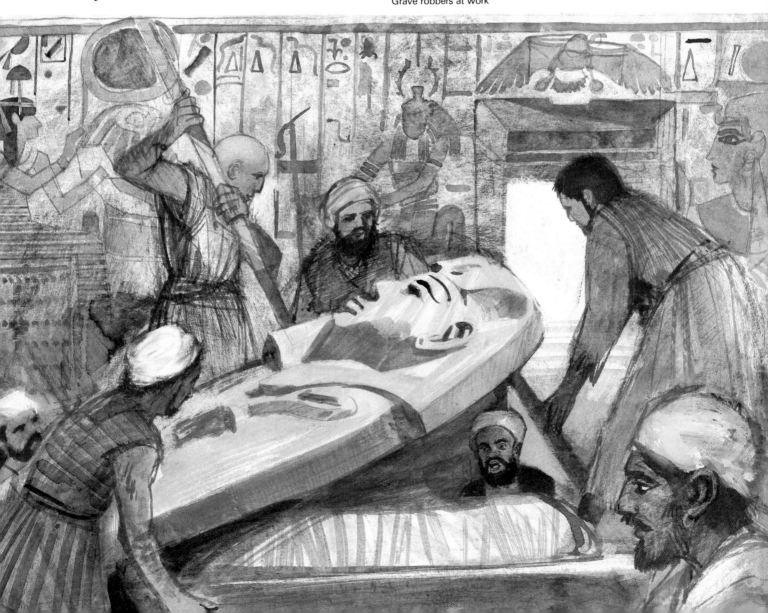

Section 6 *Egypt*

Paper, ink, hieroglyphics

A boy learning to be a scribe in ancient Egypt had to go to a special school – probably one attached to a temple and run by priests. If it was nearby he would be a day boy; if not he would have to live away from home.

It took many years to learn all the signs – there were several hundred of them. Some signs were alphabetic (like our own letters), some were pictures of the thing the scribe wished to mention and others stood for the sound of the word or part of the word. In addition, you often had to put in a 'class indicator' sign. This came after a word and showed which group it belonged to. Thus it could be that the word was written in letters, drawn in a picture, split into parts for the sound of its syllables and followed by a symbol showing what type of word it was. All very complicated. English is not so good as Egyptian for this kind of writing but if we used the same methods for 'caterpillar', we might wind up with: CTPLR

This is supposing that the sign ☼ means the class of creepy crawly insects and similar creatures. You will have noticed that the alphabetic version uses no vowels. If we did this in our language, you wouldn't know whether 'BT' stood for 'bat', 'bet', 'bit', 'but', 'boot', 'boat', 'bought', 'beat', 'bout', or 'bait' without some other indication.

As though that were not difficult enough, Egyptian scribes sometimes wrote from left to right, sometimes from right to left and, occasionally, from top to bottom. No wonder the scientists took so long to crack the code. In addition they were faced, not only with an unknown way of writing but also an unknown language.

Their first break-through came with the discovery of an inscribed stone at Rosetta on the Nile Delta. The inscription was in both Greek and hieroglyphics (or 'sacred carvings', as these signs are known). They guessed that the names of pharaohs which they could read in the Greek part were the same as the groups of signs surrounded by a thin line. Assuming that one name was 'PTOLEMY' and another 'CLEOPATRA', it became possible to suppose that the first letter of 'Ptolemy' should be the fifth sign of 'Cleopatra' and so

The Rosetta stone

on. It was. Similarly, the sign of 'L' was also in the right place as were those for the other letters which appeared in both names.

All this is very much simplified. It's wasn't as easy as all that and took decades before much ancient Egyptian could be read.

A boy learner was given pieces to copy and he used anything that could be written on – a slab of stone, a broken pot or a plaster covered board – just so long as they could be wiped clean and reused.

Writing fluid was not really ink but more like our water colour paints. Red and black were the popular colours, made from powdered red ochre and lamp black. The powder was mixed with gum and water into a thick paste which was poured into little round pans to harden, whilst a 'pen' was made of a twig or reed, chewed into a frayed condition and then sharpened.

Paper was used for important documents. It was made from the papyrus plant. Nowadays this grows only on the banks of the upper Nile but thousands of years ago it was common along all of the river. It was cut in bundles and sent to the paper maker.

He chopped the stalks into one foot lengths, peeled off the bark and cut the inner pith into long thin slices. Some of these were laid side by side on a flat surface and others placed across them at right angles. Then the paper maker pounded them with a wooden mallet until they stuck together.

The resulting sheets were either hung up to dry and trimmed to shape, or hammered and pasted edge to edge with others to make a long strip. The longest we know of is the so-called Harris Papyrus, which is 135 feet long.

The first papyrus seems to date back to the earliest days or writing – that is to say, some 5,000 years ago – and is a humble set of temple accounts. However, as time went on, scribes ventured into the realms of verse, drama, story telling and history. The latter has proved very valuable to us in the modern world, for we now know more about ancient Egypt than any similar civilisation which never developed writing.

It's just barely possible that the idea of writing was copied by the Egyptians from the scribes in Mesopotamia. If this is true, then they took nothing but the idea: the two systems are not alike. Hieroglyphics were purely a product of the Nile valley.

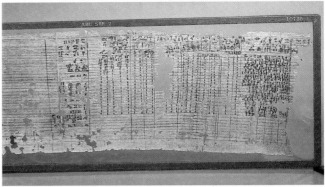
Temple accounts

Making papyrus

Practising writing

The Indus valley

No one in Europe knew about the ancient civilisation of the Indian sub-continent until the 19th century but those who lived in the land of the two rivers 4,000 years ago knew about places such as Harappa and Mohenjo-daro. These cities in the valley of the river Indus in modern Pakistan were trading with the people of Mesopotamia 2,000 years before Christ.

Harappa in our times was no more than a massive hill of ruins when it was reported to be of interest in about 1820. Many seal stones kept turning up. These had carved pictures of animals and signs in some unknown script. Some of them were published and brought to the attention of scholars.

Seal stone

The ruins didn't look very promising, as nearby towns and villages had used them as a free quarry for centuries. Even the British company that had built the Karachi to Lahore railway in 1856 had removed tons of 'hard core' for the permanent way. It wasn't until January, 1921 that Indian archaeologists began the first scientific investigations.

The discovery of the second site of the same civilisation came by chance. In 1922, another Indian scientist was working on an early Buddhist monastery, when it became obvious that its foundations were much older than the rest of the building. The ruins were called Mohenjo-daro (the Place of Death) and were excavated by Marshall and Mackay during the 1920s. Some other sites of the same type were also found.

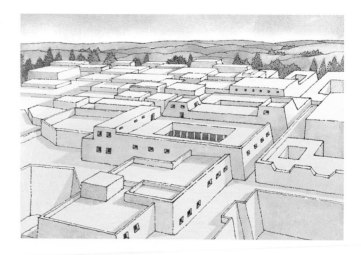

Soon, the outlines of large, well designed towns began to emerge. The houses and other buildings were made of kiln-dried, rather than mud brick, which seemed to point to a somewhat rainier climate than the modern one. The Indus was more like the rivers of Mesopotamia than the Nile. It flooded once a year, bringing down the fertile silt but it was much less easy to forecast, both as to time and amount of water. Occasionally the river rose high and violently and even changed course.

However, the region would grow crops such as wheat, barley, rice and even cotton and there were

Reconstruction of granary at Mohenjo-daro

plenty of animals to hunt or to tame. There are drawings or carvings of tigers, elephants, water buffaloes, crocodiles and rhinoceroses.

In addition, animals such as the horse, camel, sheep, goat, cow and donkey were tamed – probably long before the people lived in towns. In fact, the towns were most likely founded about 2,500 B.C., when the villages had already been in existence for a thousand years. The Indus valley civilisation is something of a mystery, as it did not apparently develop from the kind of life that went before it on the river plain. No one knows for certain how it arose, but at about 2000 B.C., the whole of north west India was sprinkled with towns, all seemingly laid out by the same designers.

There were well built two storey houses enclosing wells, private bathrooms and lavatories, with earthenware pipes to carry the waste out to neat, brick-lined drains, all equipped with inspection holes at regular intervals. There doesn't seem to have been a single grand temple but at Mohenjo-daro a large bath for some sort of religious bathing was discovered.

Another prominent feature was the citadel with high walls and towers. Many Indus valley towns show extensive remains of huge granaries. At Mohenjo-daro, the unloading bay for the carts was identified. Grain seems to have been brought to the store by boat at Harappa.

So far, not much in the way of art has turned up although there were some quite good statues and figurines. The best work is seen on the stone seals carved with animals that have been appearing for over a century.

These animal pictures are accompanied by signs in an unknown script. It's strange that the three most important ancient civilisations should each have produced its own special way of writing. The cuneiform of Mesopotamia and the hieroglyphics of Egypt finally gave up their secrets and we can now read what the ancient people wrote.

Unfortunately, the Indus valley inscriptions are too short and too scarce for much progress to be made. There are no long rock-cut inscriptions, nor lengths of papyrus. The pieces we have may be nothing more than proper names – we just don't know. And, of course, the biggest barrier to breaking the code is that we haven't the faintest idea of what language the people spoke. So, even if we were lucky enough to find a sort of Indian Rosetta stone, it wouldn't be much good to us.

The life of the cities seems to have come to an end some time between 1750 and 1500 B.C. We don't know why but there are several possibilities. Did the soil become less fertile? Were trees and other natural resources exhausted? Was the soil washed away by floods? Was there a revolution against a too severe government? Were they invaded?

It's true that the houses had begun to decay and ones which were little more than hovels were built on top of the remains. As the decay went on, the cities were slowly turning into slums. In the upper layers of Mohenjo-daro, the archaeologists found several skeletons showing signs of a violent death.

In extent, the Indus valley civilisation was far larger and more uniform than that of either Mesopotamia or Egypt: it didn't start until they had been going for a thousand years and it finished when they still had about another thousand years to run.

China

Most people who are interested in history seem to know something about China in prehistoric times. They've heard of Peking Man who lived half a million years ago and is the first human being known to have used fire. They may also have heard of the discovery of old stone age tools together with the remains of modern man, dating back to 30,000 B.C. Not so many know of China's middle stone age, traces of which have turned up in the northern frontier region, in the south and south west, as well as on the island of Taiwan.

We find new stone age settlements appearing in the north and north west, dating from about 4,000 B.C. Here, along the river valleys, the soil was particularly well suited to the primitive farming that was done. The name 'Yang-shao' is applied to these people, who still probably relied more on hunting and fishing than they did on growing things. Their houses had low walls on a round or rectangular pattern, topped off with a roof of thatch and clay which may have reached the ground all round the dwelling. They knew nothing of metal and had only flint tools and weapons.

It seems that the various farming peoples who lived along the valleys of Chinese rivers existed very much as the dwellers in ancient Egypt and Mesopotamia must have done and had many of the same problems to solve.

The discovery of bronze goes back to about 1600 B.C. which also roughly marks the beginning of the first historical period. It is known as the Shang. A kind of picture writing, not very different from its modern forms seems to have developed at about the same time.

The rule of the Shang kings lasted about 500 years until they were conquered by a people known as the Chou. The area they controlled gradually increased to include a good deal of what we think of as modern China. Their capital was at first at or near Hsi-an.

Among the features of their civilisation were **1.** The beginnings of social classes **2.** Burials with rich grave goods and human sacrifice **3.** War chariots **4.** Growth of towns. The use of bronze and a system of writing have already been mentioned. The rule of the Chou collapsed into civil wars until 246 B.C. when the self-styled first Emperor of China, Ch'in-Shih-huang-ti, came to power.

He laid the foundations of a united China in language, religion, systems of weights and measures and government, many of which have lasted until modern times. He was responsible for ordering his general, Meng T'ien to build the Great Wall.

The Great Wall of China

According to the historian of the court, one of the emperor's first acts was to start planning his own tomb. Three quarters of a million labourers were assembled to dig it out. The burial chamber was to be filled with miniature buildings, precious stones, storage jars, small scale rivers (to be imitated with mercury), models of the heavens and the earth. Whale oil lamps were to give illumination and crossbows were fixed and cocked to fire automatically at tomb robbers.

When the emperor died, the second emperor ordered all his father's womenfolk to be buried with him. Then someone suggested that the skilled workmen knew too much about the tomb they had constructed, so orders were given that they too should be shut up alive in the grave. As far as we know, robbers don't seem to have done much damage and in 1985, excavators have found the walls surrounding the burial chamber. They also found a high level of mercury in the soil – perhaps the remains of the model rivers?

Less than a mile and a half away, one of the greatest tomb discoveries ever made came to light in March 1974. It was in that year that the local people decided to sink wells to improve their water supply. The diggers suddenly came across a life-sized pottery figure which looked as though it had been there for some time. According to the museum authorities who were then called in, it had.

It was the first one of some 7,000 buried soldier-statues which had lain in the earth since the funeral of Ch'in-Shih-huang-ti, although they were not mentioned in the history.

By digging here and there, archaeologists established that the original pit was almost 700 feet long and nearly 200 feet wide. It had eleven parallel corridors packed with life-sized model soldiers – each corridor with over 600 men except the two narrower outside ones. In six of the passages were chariots drawn by four horses. Men were arranged in long lines, three abreast, across the short sides. There were ramps leading up to the surface at each end. Even six years after the first discovery, no more than 2% of the 'grave' has been dug up.

A second pit turned up in May, 1976 with another 1400 statues, mostly cavalry and charioteers. A month later, the archaeologists found the army's headquarters staff in a third grave. A fourth pit was empty, although, like the others, it had brick pavements and wooden roofs.

The labour represented by these 7,000 soldier figures was enormous. To start with, they were not pressed from moulds – no two are exactly alike and even the faces are different. Most of the arms are real weapons; some of the swords were still razor sharp. Each statue had been carefully painted in one of several colour combinations, for example, black shoes, blue trousers and green cloaks. The armour, which consisted of many little metal plates, was painted black with white rivets.

In the nearby museum are specimen warriors and a restored chariot. The locals think that other pits may yet be found. Even if they are not, this private army for a dead emperor must rank with the great archaeological discoveries of all time.

The Emperor's warriors and horses at Xi-an

The Hittites

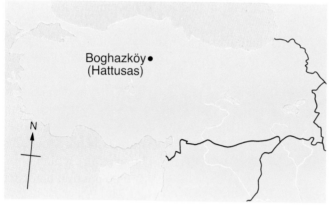

Turkey

Pass at Boghazköy

Just over a hundred years ago, the name 'Hittite' was almost unknown, apart from one or two references in the Bible. Then, in 1880, an Englishman named Sayce said that in his opinion, a number of rock carvings in modern Turkey and further south were the visible remains of a long forgotten empire – that of the Hittites. He was proved right. In 1906 a large number of clay tablets was unearthed at a place called Boghazköy.

The tablets were mostly in the wedge-shaped signs of Mesopotamia and some could be read without too much difficulty. Others, although looking like straightforward cuneiform, turned out to be in an unknown language. There were also inscriptions in a kind of picture writing. It took many years before it became possible to decipher the picture writing. The decipherers were helped when some stone pillars with messages carved on them were found at Karatepe. There were two languages, Hittite and Phoenician, the latter being already known. The columns were rather like the Rosetta stone in Egypt, giving the decoders more new symbols and their meanings. It had long been suspected that Hittite might belong to the same group of languages as the ancestors of most modern European ones – including English. Now the scholars could make out 'WÄDAR' and 'EZZATENI' and translate them as 'water' and 'eat'.

They also found out that the place where the first tablets were found was in fact called Hattusas at about 1600 B.C. and was the capital of the ancient empire of the Hittites. Much else came to light.

Hattusas had a fortified citadel and massive surrounding walls over two miles long. The Hittites claimed that it was one of the cities taken by their half legendary kings, Pithanas, and his son, Anittas. A few other conquered towns can be identified – enough to show that at its greatest extent, the whole of Anatolia (mostly modern Turkey) had been overrun with Syria, the western coast of Turkey, much of the Holy Land, Cyprus and a good deal of northern Mesopotamia.

One Hittite king made a surprise attack down the Euphrates in 1595 B.C. and captured Babylon. Another, Suppiluliumash, was such a great conqueror that the widow of Tutankhamen wrote him an official letter asking that one of his sons to be sent to Egypt to marry her.

Ordinary Hittites were of medium height, thickset and with bony noses. They wore felt boots and short, belted kilts. Some were bearded and others clean shaven. They grew barley and wheat and raised sheep and goats.

Like most ancient peoples, they worshipped numerous gods, the chief of which was Teshup, a sort of middle eastern Thor, for he is shown as holding a hammer and a flash of lightning. Like Thor, he was the god of the storm. His wife was the goddess of the sun.

One of the secrets of Hittite military success was their use of iron for weapons. Before 1400 B.C., it was known that some red minerals (e.g. iron oxide) would reduce to metal at temperatures not much above those for producing molten copper from blue and green ores. But iron will only flow like copper or lead in much hotter fires, a process which was not to be invented for nearly another 3000 years.

The Hittite method was repeated heatings and hammerings to drive out the rock impurities. If you were lucky and had a little natural carbon in your iron ore, you got a very good metal from which to make swords. The knowledge of how to do this wasn't available to the rest of the world until the collapse of the Hittite empire in about 1200 B.C.

Just before this happened, Muwatallis, the Hittite king, claimed a great battle victory against the Egyptians. Rameses II, the Egyptian leader, also claimed to have won, as his numerous monuments bear witness. The battle was probably a draw. It was the last great engagement of the Hittite army with its light, spoke-wheeled and horse-drawn chariots. Great movements of peoples in the middle east only a lifetime later led to the disappearance of the Hittite empire.

Some of the old provincial city states survived for a few more centuries, for example Carchemish, Malatya and Karatepe. It was probably one of these small shadowy Hittite kingdoms to which the Bible refers in the story of Abraham.

Five hundred years after the destruction of the capital, Hatussas, the last traces of the Hittites disappeared from history.

Hittites

Walls at Hattusas

The Hebrews

Man working on Dead Sea Scrolls

In a laboratory in Israel a man is carefully cutting into pieces an ancient looking roll of thin copper plate. We would like to know what he is doing. He tells us.

'This is one of the Dead Sea scrolls,' he says. 'There are many of them, some written on linen – all more than 1900 years old. They are mostly religious texts – parts of what you would call "The Old Testament," he adds with a smile.

'The Bible tells the story of the Jewish people, the Children of Israel, as we call ourselves. It's strange that a people so small in numbers and so beset with enemies has survived. Our first ancestors lived long ago – as far in the past to the writers of these scrolls as the writers are to us.'

'That must be about 4000 years?'

'Something like that, yes. One of our earliest heroes was named Abraham. He is supposed to have been born in Sumer at a place called Ur. We were a nomadic people, keeping goats and sheep and always shifting about. We travelled slowly and over the centuries we gradually moved up the Euphrates and into Canaan, our promised land. Some of us crossed the desert into pharaoh's empire and many of us did well in Egypt. This must have been roughly about 1700 B.C. and things might have gone on like this for a very long time. But then a pharaoh (who may have been Rameses II) made life so hard for us that, after a series of adventures, we escaped from Egypt altogether.

'Under our leader, Moses, we once more became wandering shepherds with tents of woven goat's hair. We spent forty years in the Sinai desert and began to forget our covenant with God until Moses showed us the holy laws he had received from the Lord on Mount Sinai.'

'The ten commandments?'

'That's right. These rules kept us together – that and the fact that we had only one god to worship. Mind you, Akhenaten tried to bring in a religion with only one deity. He might have been more sympathetic towards us had we stayed. However –' he shrugs.

'We left Egypt in about 1280 B.C. and started the conquest of Canaan forty years later. Moses was dead by then and Joshua had taken his place. You may know the story of how Joshua's trumpeters marched round the first enemy city they came to, blowing their rams-horn trumpets. The walls of Jericho definitely fell, as the Bible tells us but archaeologists have found traces of an earthquake, which God probably used to carry out his will.

'Anyway, in fifteen years the tribes of Israel had settled all over Canaan, or Palestine as it was sometimes known – from the Philistines who also lived there. You've heard of David and Goliath? Samson and Delilah? Well, both Delilah and Goliath were Philistines.

'David came to the throne about 1012 B.C., succeeding Saul, our first king. Then there was Solomon, our most magnificent ruler. He had hundreds of wives and thousands of slaves. He had many gorgeous palaces made and it was he who ordered the building of the Temple in Jerusalem.

'Sargon II of Assyria captured Samaria in 721 B.C. and carried its people off into slavery. He had an inscription made. It's still in existence and gives the exact number of Jewish prisoners – 27,280! Even this wasn't the biggest disaster. Nebuchadrezzar and his Babylonian armies conquered Jerusalem itself in 587 B.C. They smashed the temple on the hill of Zion and marched hundreds of thousands of captives off to Mesopotamia. There they stayed for nearly fifty years until Babylon itself was taken by the Persians under King Cyrus and they were freed. But you can read most of this in your own Bible.'

'Tell us more about the Dead Sea scrolls.'

'They were found in a cave near the Dead Sea by a young Arab boy. He'd gone into the cave to look for a stray goat when he found these rolls of manuscript in pottery jars. They were brought to the attention of the authorities and we're now carefully unrolling and studying them.

'They seem to have been owned by a community of monks called Essenes. The remains of their monastery are still to be seen at the foot of the nearby cliffs.

'One of these copper rolls tells an incredible story. Whilst most of them are the oldest versions of books in the Bible yet known, this one tells where the monks hid their valuables – treasures given by friends and supporters and any possessions the monks themselves had once owned. The total of gold and silver tucked away is stated to be an unbelievable 160 tons! I'm afraid none of it has ever been found. If it ever was there, it's gone now.

'Of course, far more valuable than that are the religions. The middle east, you know, has produced three of the great world religions: Judaism, Christianity and Islam. Don't forget that your Christ was a Jew.'

Reconstruction of the monastery of the Essenes

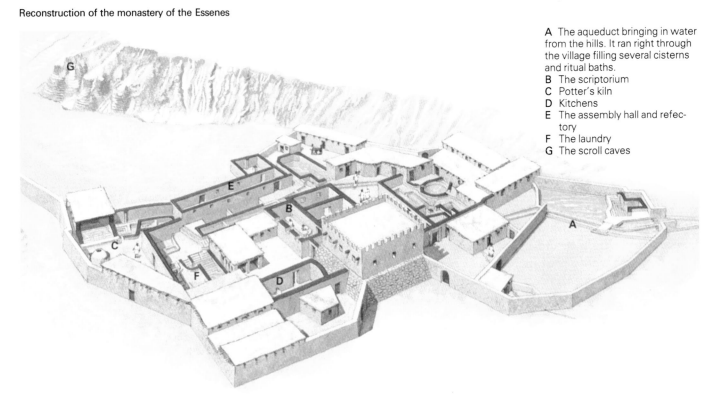

A The aqueduct bringing in water from the hills. It ran right through the village filling several cisterns and ritual baths.
B The scriptorium
C Potter's kiln
D Kitchens
E The assembly hall and refectory
F The laundry
G The scroll caves

The Assyrians

Assyria

The Assyrians were a hard, war-like people. They began to emerge as a world power by about 1350 B.C. There was a period of chaos after the Hittite empire collapsed but by 1115 B.C., when Tiglath-Pileser I became king, Assyria was a mighty country once more, with flourishing trade protected by a strong army. When Assyria and Egypt exchanged ambassadors, the pharaoh sent the Assyrians an interesting present – a live crocodile.

By the mid tenth century B.C. no one could withstand the Assyrian armies and the land itself was like a huge military camp. Every man had to be able to use weapons, a store of which was kept in the citadels of the chief cities. If he were rich, he had to supply his own arms – a bow and arrows, a nail-studded club, a spear, an axe or even a horse-drawn chariot. The cavalry rode both horses and camels.

There was an efficient corps of spies who reported regularly to the king, so he knew where and when to attack. He could then order his men to fight a battle or besiege a city, an art at which they were experts.

The army made a fortified camp near the town they were attacking and the engineers set about assembling their assault machines – scaling ladders, battering rams, armoured carts and assault towers. It was an Assyrian idea to make such machines so that they could be taken to pieces for crossing rivers or difficult, mountain country. Even the chariots might be carried as parts on pack animals. One piece of Assyrian art shows their soldiers swimming a river in full kit but staying afloat by means of air-filled leather bags. Without them they would have drowned for they wore heavy leather boots and chain mail. When the men had got over the walls or smashed holes in them with battering rams they quickly disposed of the enemy, some prisoners being impaled or beheaded. Loot was then loaded onto captured baggage wagons and the town burnt to the ground. High officials who had been spared were made to march barefoot back to Assyria, often with the severed heads of their leaders slung round their necks.

Assurnasirpal was a great conqueror. He extended Assyria's boundaries in all directions, campaigning down the river valleys and to the Mediterranean coasts. He used the spoils of war to build several palaces, including an enormous one at the modern Nimrud. The throne room alone was over 7,000 square feet in area and had to be approached through a gate flanked by the typically Assyrian statues of bulls with human heads, each with a carefully curled beard. The statues weighed thirty or forty tons apiece and were probably ferried along the Tigris to the palace in the very large coracles that were common in those days.

It was under Assurnasirpal that Assyria gained a thoroughly deserved reputation for ruthlessness and cruelty. It was his successors who pushed the empire to its greatest limits. Tiglath-Pileser, Sargon II, Sennacherib and Esarhaddon between them besieged Jerusalem, captured Babylon, drove out the pharaoh and occupied Egypt.

Esarhaddon's son, Assurbanipal, attacked Thebes and tried to destroy its colossal temples. He carried off two large Eyptian obelisks to his palace at Nineveh. It seemed that the Assyrian empire would last for ever but Assurbanipal was becoming more interested in his vast library at Nineveh than in the army. There were more than 20,000 clay tablets copied from all over the empire. (These, by the way, were later to provide archaeologists with a valuable key to life in Mesopotamia.) The king liked nothing so much as to browse among his 'books' and then discuss them with scholars. He reigned from 669 to 626 B.C., but even in his lifetime, the empire had begun to show cracks.

In 652 B.C. his brother led a revolt of neighbouring nations which was crushed within four years. It was Assyria's last successful campaign. A year after his death, Assurbanipal's sons quarrelled over who should be the next king. While they argued, Babylon rose in rebellion once more. Under their leader, Nabopolassar, father of Nebuchadrezzar, the Babylonians joined forces with the Medes and threw off Assyrian rule. They did more – their victorious soldiers chased the defeated enemy back to Nineveh, which they captured in 612 B.C. So much treasure was looted, the amounts were uncountable and the Assyrian capital was left in heaps of smoking ruins.

Dust drifted over the dead ashes and even the sites of the Assyrian palaces were forgotten, until they were dug up again in the nineteenth century. Among the finds at Assur, an earlier capital, was a fine piece of low relief sculpture, showing a charming family scene. Assurbanipal and his wife are eating an outdoor meal at a table surrounded by grape vines. Servants bring food and cool them with fans. This picture of domestic bliss is shattered in characteristic Assyrian fashion – in the background there is a severed human head hanging from one of the trees!

The Persians

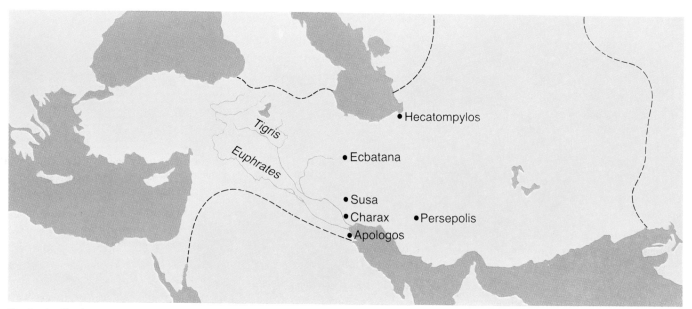

The Persian Empire

The Persian empire was the largest the world had seen. It was also one of the shortest lived. It burst upon the scene in about 550 B.C., filling the space left by the collapse of the Assyrian empire. Under its emperors, Cyrus, Cambyses, Darius and Xerxes, it was extended from eastern Europe through the Asian middle east to the banks of the Indus in modern Pakistan and south to the ancient kingdoms of Babylonia and Egypt. But in just over two centuries it was all over. What had happened?

Cyrus beat the king of the Medes in battle and took him prisoner. This was important for it was the Medes who had taken over what was left of the Assyrian empire. Cyrus then began to look westward towards Greece and the rest of Europe. Only Lydia stood in his way. Croesus, king of Lydia, was believed by his contemporaries to be the richest king who had ever lived. He had made the mistake of consulting the oracle at Delphi to decide whether to make war on Persia or not. The oracle told him that if he went to war he would 'destroy a great empire'. Gleefully, Croesus made his preparations, unaware that the oracle's pronouncements could nearly always be given more than one meaning. Croesus went to war. He did, indeed, 'destroy a great empire'. Unfortunately, it was his own!

Cyrus used the wealth from the Lydian gold mines to set up a military expedition to Babylon. He and his men attacked at night. So as to make full use of the surprise, he had previously ordered his engineers to divert the river which protected one wall. Thus, he and his infantry were able to creep along a dry river bed and attack where they were not expected.

The conquests of Cyrus were not held down with Assyrian cruelty and force – the beaten peoples were often allowed to keep their own religions and languages, even their own rulers, provided that tribute was sent regularly.

Cambyses was not so kind as his father Cyrus but in his short seven year reign, he enlarged the empire by beating Phoenicia, Egypt and the island of Cyprus. The next ruler was his son, Darius, who further expanded the boundaries towards Southern Russia, India & Northern Greece. He landed a large army at Marathon with the object of conquering Greece. This is the origin of the 'Marathon' run, for a Greek was sent at his fastest pace to warn the Spartans. The Persians were soundly defeated by a small Athenian army and Darius never got another chance. Shortly after starting the building of the great Persian capital at Persepolis in 486 B.C., he died.

Other Persian building achievements included a good network of fine roads, one of which ran for over 1500 miles. It was said that messengers using relays of horses could travel from one end of the empire to the other in just under a fortnight – extremely fast for those days.

One of the first decisions of King Xerxes was to do what his father Darius had been unable to do – to conquer Greece. He built up a large army and fleet and tried out a brand new idea. A bridge of boats was constructed by his Phoenician allies running from Asia to Europe across the Hellespont. The boats were anchored and tied side by side. Planks were laid from vessel to vessel. Then the army began to cross: it took a week of night and day operations to get them all over.

Eventually they captured Athens in 480 B.C. However, the remaining Greeks engaged the Persian fleet – all one thousand of them – at the battle of Salamis. Although the Greek ships were outnumbered by more than three to one, they outmanoeuvred the Persians and routed them. Xerxes withdrew from the Greek campaigns and spent the rest of his life adding to the beautiful city of Persepolis.

'Persepolis' is actually a Greek word meaning 'City of the Persians,' and was probably applied during the time of Alexander the Great.

Alexander crossed into Asia and defeated the last Persian emperor, Darius III at the battle of Gaugamela which means 'camel field'. The Persian ruler fled from the battle but was stabbed to death by one of his own men.

Alexander was usually generous towards his defeated enemies and never allowed his men to sack a town they had taken. In the case of Persepolis, he seems to have had a change of mind. Either that, or a terrible accident resulted in a disastrous fire, during which Persepolis was burnt to the ground. Only a few columns and sculptured stones standing at the head of splendid staircases serve to remind us of the largest empire of those times.

The Phoenicians

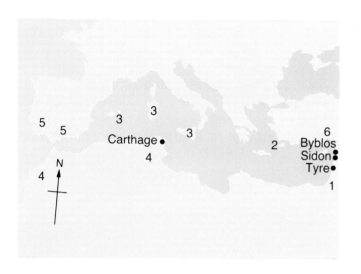

Unlike the majority of the ancient peoples we have looked at so far, the Phoenicians were not really warlike, nor did they have what anyone could call an empire. They lived in a coastal strip of what is now northern Israel and Lebanon and their chief cities were Tyre, Sidon and Byblos. The area was no more than 200 miles long and as little as fifteen miles across.

Because it was a poor region, the Phoenicians turned their attention away from the land and became Mediterranean sailors. After the Minoans, they were the great traders and seafarers of the ancient world.

Trireme

Their ships were biremes and triremes, driven by a rectangular sail on a single mainmast, provided the wind was right, and by banks of oars if it wasn't. They bought cheaply in one place and sold dear in another but always took most cargo space for their own products.

They were excellent craftsmen in copper, silver and gold jewellery; they carved ivory and turned pottery. They were fine woodworkers and knew how to decorate their other wares with coloured glass. They exported a purple dye got from a local shellfish which became the colour of authority and power. In Rome, only the emperor could wear, or even afford to wear, purple robes.

The Phoenicians had cut down and sold overseas huge quantities of building timber, particularly the cedar trees which grew in abundance on the hillsides. As early as 2700 B.C. they had sent wood to Egypt to be used in the royal funeral ship (see pp. 84–85). Solomon's great Temple at Jerusalem was partly constructed from the cedars of Lebanon.

They ventured farther and farther afield until they had trading posts or colonies all round the Mediterranean, for example: 1. the southern coast of Palestine   2. the islands of Rhodes and Cyprus   3. Sicily, Sardinia and the Balearic islands   4. almost half the north African coast including the Atlantic shore of what is now Morocco   5. southern Spain and Portugal   6. south east Turkey. There is a tradition that they visited Cornwall or the Scilly islands in search of tin but there is little evidence for this. Cadiz in Spain was founded in the 12th century B.C. At about 800 B.C.,

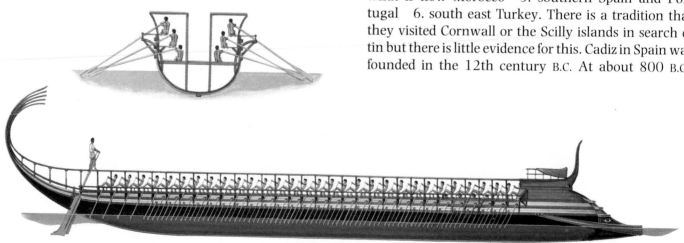

Carthage began as a colony (near modern day Tunis) and grew to be the largest and most important Phoenician city of all.

Signs of their religious life can be seen in the temples of their homeland. In Byblos, for example, a temple contained a double row of gold capped obelisks. We also know the names of some of their gods. They worshipped Baal and Astarte as the chief god and his consort: Teshub and Tanith were revered, particularly in Carthage and Baal Amon, their African god, apparently insisted that children were sacrificed to him.

From illustrations of the time we know that the ordinary Phoenician wore a white ankle length tunic with swathes of purple edged cloth wound round the body on top of the tunic, or a short kilt with a long overall like garment as outer wear. The men had beards but 'moustaches only' were rare: they wore their hair long, bunched at the back and kept in place with a narrow head band.

One of their legends says that Phoenician ships started from the Gulf of Suez, sailed south right round Africa, up the west coast and back home through the Pillars of Hercules (Straits of Gibraltar) and into the Mediterranean. They claimed to have observed the Tyrian Cynosure (Pole Star) getting lower in the sky each night until it disappeared completely – evidence enough, surely, that the sailors had indeed gone right round Africa.

But perhaps their chief claim to fame was the invention of the first successful alphabet. There had been alphabets before – even the Egyptians wrote the names of their pharaohs in a sort of alphabet. But it was the clever Phoenicians who took picture writing and

Phoenician traders

made from it a system for every day, where one sign always stood for one sound. From henceforth, all a learner had to do was to master two or three dozen symbols, in place of the several thousand that had to be committed to memory before.

They took this invention to their colonies and trading areas, whence it passed to the Greeks and Romans, and through them to the rest of the world. From Syria it moved eastward and became the ancestor of modern Arabic script. No one is very sure how the symbols of hieroglyphics were changed into letters but perhaps the following is not far from the truth: ⌇, an ox head, alters to ⌀ because it was quicker to write and then to ⋉, which is even quicker. Phoenicians wrote it ⋉ and the Greeks and Romans changed its attitude to the more familiar A. If the Phoenicians had never done anything else, this would have been enough to put us in their debt and to secure their place in history.

Phoenician ivory carving

The first farmers

On pp.44–45 we saw how hunting tribes gradually changed into farming tribes. The important word is 'gradually'. The gathering of wild plant products had always been done but what was happening here was that these products were slowly becoming a larger and larger part of the tribe's diet, until, thousands of years ago Man learned how to grow the plants to order, where and when he wanted them.

The discovery of plant and animal farming was made in western Asia, where the ancestors of domestic crops and beasts had once been wild. Several thousand years went by between the discovery of farming and the arrival of the first farmers in Britain. The reason for the delay isn't hard to find. No farmer in the middle east ever said to himself, 'Let's go and farm in Britain.' Of course not. People planted seeds and if the harvest was good they stayed in the same place, perhaps for decades, or until the plant foods in the soil were all used up. When that happened, the harvest would no longer feed everyone, so they moved on to a new spot and began again.

As populations got larger, it became harder to find fresh areas suitable for growing food. Families moved bit by bit into south east Europe and along its southern coasts to Greece, Italy, Spain and France. They also inched their way up the valleys of the great rivers such as the Danube. It took centuries for the new ideas to spread.

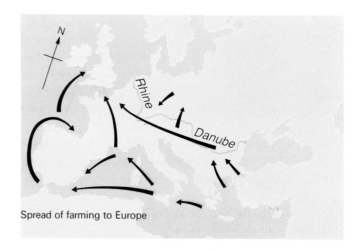

Spread of farming to Europe

Finally, by about three or four thousand years B.C. or perhaps even a little earlier, the first farmers arrived in Britain. They probably came from France and crossed the Channel at its narrowest place. The Channel was not nearly so wide in those days for the winter storms had not yet washed away so much of the cliffs on both sides.

The likeliest craft for the crossing were wooden framed boats covered with waterproofed animal skins. These would have taken the human beings with their bags of seed corn and also a few young animals with which they could start stock farming.

Britain must have been forested or marshy nearly all over, so they had to choose places not so thickly wooded. Then they began to cut down trees and burn the undergrowth. Oxen could be used to haul out the stumps. They planted their seeds and pastured their cattle on the plentiful grass. As well as cattle, they had sheep, goats, pigs and pet dogs. They grew wheat, barley and possibly flax. The latter was almost certainly for its oily seeds as the ideas of spinning and weaving linen, or wool for that matter, were still to come and our pioneers made do with clothing of soft leather and furs.

Cutting down trees needed keen edged implements – not the clumsy hand axes of the old stone age but smooth, sharp chopping tools, either home-made of local flint or got in exchange for food products. These 'foreign' axes could have come from as far away as Land's End, Wales or Langdale Pike in the Lake District, where there were clans which did little else but manufacture tools and weapons of stone.

As to the earliest farmers – very few traces of their houses have yet been found. For a long time it was thought they had lived in what are called 'causewayed cattle camps' such as the ones at Windmill Hill in Wiltshire, or Yeoveney near Staines in Middlesex. However, we now know that these earthwork circles were used for the autumn round-up of cattle. Grass doesn't grow in the winter so the beasts had to be collected together and most of them slaughtered before the cold weather was really under way. The earliest definite new stone age house remains have been found at Carn Brea in Cornwall and the cattle camps can't ever have been permanent homes.

Another change in the landscape made by the new stone age farmers was the building of large mounds of earth to house the dead. In the early days, the corpse or corpses were put inside a wooden structure which was then heaped over with soil. Later, they learned to make 'long barrows', as they are known, from 'trilithons' of stone.

Now, when the earth was piled up, the stone didn't collapse as wood eventually did. The grave could be sealed by rolling a boulder across the end of the stone-built passage and opened every time there was a new funeral.

We don't know what language they spoke or what they called themselves but they were the first people in Britain to farm, the first to use proper pottery and the first to wield really smooth stone tools and weapons.

West Kennett long barrow

Skara Brae

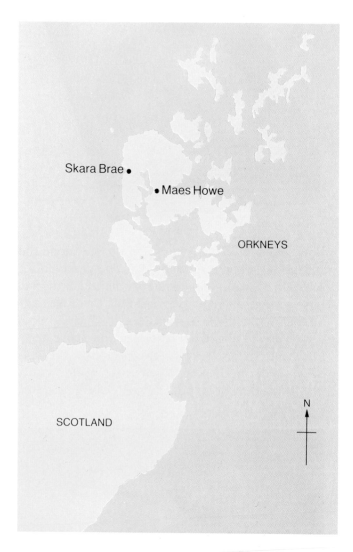

In the last spread we read about the first farmers in Britain. They arrived here before Egypt was united and before the building of the first pyramid. During the same period and at a time when Abraham was still hundreds of years in the future, a strange people built a strange village in the Orkney Isles to the north of Scotland.

Again, because they neither read nor wrote, we don't know who they were nor even the name they used for themselves as a group. Let's ask an archaeologist to tell us what is known about them.

'It's difficult,' he says, 'without any written records. We can only go on the actual things they left behind.

This is not an easy task. If you don't believe me, take a look around your own house or school. How much will still be in existence 5,000 years from now? (That's how old these remains are). Remember that glass and china may survive, plus some metal and stone but little else. What could a future archaeologist say about you, if all he had was a couple of tea cups, some shards of window glass, a bottle opener and a set of knives and forks?

'Anyway, let's begin at the beginning and see what we know and what we can guess. We must go back to a severe storm over the north of Scotland in the winter of 1850. The gale whipped up huge waves which crashed into Skara Brae on the coast of Mainland, the most important island of the Orkneys. Parts of the sand dunes collapsed, revealing what seemed to be a rubbish dump underneath. It was fifteen feet high and consisted mainly of ashes, although there were also some sea-shells, bits of horn, bone and half burnt wood.

'Eleven years later, the first proper dig was organised. It uncovered stone walled enclosures and passageways. In the next few years there were more digs. The pattern began to emerge of a small village. By 1867 four huts had been cleared and a number of stone implements recovered.

'Apart from some fairly aimless digging in 1913, nothing more was done until 1924, when the site was put under government protection. A lot of good that did!'

'Why do you say that?'

'Because a year later, another bad storm swept away some of the rubbish heap and part of the stone walling. They had to build sea defences to keep the site safe. While the building was going on, Gordon Childe made some important discoveries. Much of what we know we owe to him. It wasn't until 1973 though, that we got any reliable information about the date.

'There were nine stone built houses altogether. One was roofed in stone, the others had been thatched, perhaps with turf. The passages between them were paved and also roofed with stone slabs. The largest hut was about twenty feet square. Most of them were well furnished, with a hearth stone, wall cupboards, a stone table, bed spaces and even a sideboard or dresser.

Skara Brae as it is now (above) and as it was (below)

'The village seems to have been occupied on several different occasions. The earliest people must have lived here before the first pharaoh ruled in Egypt. From the rubbish we can tell that they ate mutton, lamb and beef, whereas the later squatters, if we can call them that, ate shellfish and wild deer meat. Were the first settlers wise men, perhaps? Did they come here from somewhere else in Europe? Did they bring a new religion with them? No one knows but maybe there's some truth in all these guesses. For not far away there are two stone circles of about the same age as the village. These 'henges', as they are called, are almost certainly temples, whatever else they may be. Perhaps our wise men preached a new religion and got the locals to put up the stone circles.

'It could be that they taught the natives how to build in stone. Skara Brae village is made and furnished entirely from stone slabs. Maes Howe, in the same neighbourhood, is a magnificent stone burial chamber. It's thirteen feet high inside and is constructed by laying stone courses one on the other until the roof line is reached. Then the slabs are pushed slightly inwards. This was done with each succeeding layer, piling earth up on the outside to stop them over-balancing and falling in. Finally the space left is small enough to be covered with a single roofing slab.

'Of course, we don't know if they were missionaries but it's an interesting idea.'

Silbury, Avebury and Stonehenge

Silbury

This artificial hillock looks a bit like one of the mottes the Normans used as bases for their castles, albeit an outsize one. It was never a base for anything as far as we know. It's a lot bigger than a castle mound and a lot older, dating back to well before 2000 B.C.

It was quite an eerie experience to walk down a tunnel dug by the Welsh School of Mining and to see chalky, earthen sides that no other human eyes had seen for over 4000 years. It seems terribly mysterious but at prehistoric ground level in the centre of the mound there is absolutely nothing – no burial, no monument – nothing

It is 130 feet high and covers 5¼ acres. The labour involved must have been enormous. It has been worked out that several million man hours would have been needed to build it. Considering that the toilers had no more than deer antler pickaxes, ox shoulder-blade shovels and perhaps leather bags for carting away the dirt, it's not surprising that it probably took several years to pile up from the surrounding ditch.

Avebury

There are something like 700 prehistoric stone circles in the British Isles: this is the largest. The huge ditch encloses 28½ acres and is about 1400 feet in diameter. There is room inside for almost four Stonehenges in a straight line and the actual area is nearly 19 times as large as Stonehenge.

The ditch is half silted up and the outer bank overgrown with grass. Once the ditch was 30 feet deep and 40 feet wide at the top, with a bank of gleaming white chalk.

Around the inner edge of the ditch once stood nearly a hundred huge, rough sarsen blocks of stone. Only a few are left. There were four entrances, some with 'avenues' leading away from Avebury but these seem to have been added a good deal later.

Originally, there were two smaller stone circles inside the large one. These smaller circles are only just smaller than the one at Stonehenge. Few of the stones are still in position.

Stonehenge

The most important and impressive stone circle in Europe, probably in the world, was not erected all at once. In fact, the building was spread over at least a thousand years, from the late neolithic to the bronze age.

In the new stone age, the workmen made a bank and ditch around a circle measuring 380 feet across. Just outside the ring stood a single rough sarsen called the 'Heel Stone'. Inside the ditch a ring of 56 small holes was dug and almost immediately filled in again. Some of them contained the remains of human cremations. They are today marked with cement discs and are known as 'Aubrey Holes'.

At various dates, rings and horseshoe-shapes of dressed stones were put up, taken down and re-erected in other positions. Some of the stones came from only a short distance away but others were rafted and dragged on rollers from South Wales, well over a hundred miles away, even if you take a direct line. Again, the labour required to haul these massive slabs, some in excess of 30 tonnes, can well be imagined.

Today, although in ruins, Stonehenge has enough stones remaining for us to imagine the complete pattern. There were five 'trilithons' (Greek = 'three stones' – two uprights with a lintel across the top) arranged in the shape of a horseshoe at the centre. Then comes a circle of single standing bluestones, imported from Wales.

The outer ring is the most interesting. It consists of a circle of 13 feet high sarsens with lintel stones on top, once forming a continuous ring. The lintels are morticed and tenoned to the uprights and tongued and grooved to each other.

No one knows for sure how the building was done – perhaps the stones were levered up on a timber frame with long poles and ropes. No one knows why it was put up either, although all kinds of ideas have been suggested. Some people think it was a kind of observatory and it's true that certain stones are in line with important sun, moon or star positions. This could have enabled the wise men to calculate dates exactly – vital to people with no writing and therefore no calendar – and thus keep track of the seasons.

Bronze age barrows

'Barrow' comes from an old English word meaning 'hill'. In the latter part of the stone age, barrows were long and low, like the typical burial place at West Kennett, just south of Silbury. But in the bronze age, graves were almost always circular. Much of what we know of the bronze age in Britain comes from these round barrows.

It's a pity we don't know more than we do. Unfortunately, many of the barrows have disappeared in modern times – the result of intensive farming, mining, building, quarrying or gravel digging. Sometimes the barrows were deliberately destroyed.

In the late 18th and early 19th centuries, gentlemen interested in the past sent their servants to see what those strange humps were which showed above ground level in parts of the estate. They were not particularly interested in the bronze age as such, they merely wished to recover ancient or valuable articles. You can imagine a gentleman of those days sitting on a camp stool, sipping a glass of wine and watching his gardeners and footmen as they dug away three or four complete barrows in a couple of days.

There must have been many such burial mounds at one time: in the West Country alone, there are records of at least 6000.

Who built them and why? It seems that the first people to make round barrows are known only from the typical pottery which they made and used. We don't know what they called themselves, so we have called them 'The Beaker People'. They appear to have been the first people in Britain to cast copper and bronze weapons, tools and ornaments. Although metal working was known in the near east as early as about 6000 B.C., it wasn't until 4000 years later that it reached these islands.

Copper came first, then it was mixed with tin to make bronze. Bronze was used for daggers, swords, chisels, and jewellery. All the same, it remained expensive and flint continued in use for centuries afterwards.

In all, the bronze age in Britain lasted for about a thousand years. During that time burial customs altered. It's quite likely that the Beaker People, at least at first, buried their dead in the same long barrows that the new stone age tribes used. Then they began to make round barrows with the general rule that every corpse should have its own barrow.

After a while it became the custom to burn the dead, either where the funeral was to be or nearby. The ashes and bones were collected and put in a clay vessel over which the earth was piled and a ditch dug around it. Towards the end of the bronze age, about 1200 B.C., the burnt remains in their urn were just put in a hole in the ground which was then filled in.

The middle phase, that of the round-barrow is the most interesting. There were several different types, called variously bowl, bell, disc, saucer or pond barrow, depending on the shape and size of the mound and ditch. They varied in size from the tiny forty footers up to, or even just over, 200 feet in diameter. It's sometimes possible to say whether a funeral was for a man or a woman from its shape and size.

We think that these graves were for the ruling classes – chieftains, their sons and other relations. As rulers, they would expect to have their earthly possessions with them in the after-life. The lucky

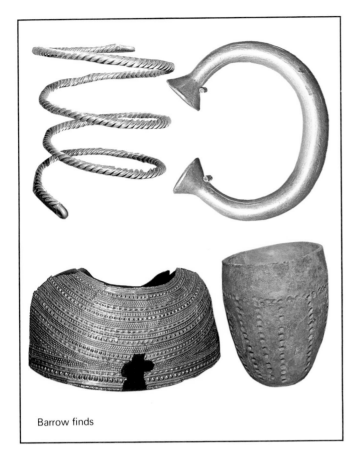

Barrow finds

Two different types of barrow

Aerial photo showing Celtic field patterns

archaeologist thus had a chance to turn up finds in a barrows that have been neither ploughed up nor robbed.

From such graves have come bronze knives, swords and daggers with gold and amber handles, earrings and cups of gold, beads of amber, jet, faience (possibly from Eygpt), shale and gold, battleaxes, the remains of clothing and shields, discs and squares of plate gold (used either as ornaments or as a display of wealth and power), a belt with a gold hook and eye fastening – even razors and trumpets have turned up.

Traces of square or rectangular fields can often be seen – in some instances carefully avoiding barrows, though we don't know very much about the *living* bronze age peoples, apart from their fields. The fields are marked on ordnance survey maps as 'Celtic Fields' or 'Strip Lynchets'. There are some faint traces of villages and single huts probably dating to the middle or late bronze age.

Some modern authorities believe that the owners of the fields and barrows may have been the ancestors of Celtic peoples such as the Welsh, driven westward by waves of iron using invaders, leaving behind them the chalk circles of their round barrows, dazzling white amid the short, green grass which was soon to cover them.

123

The coming of the iron age

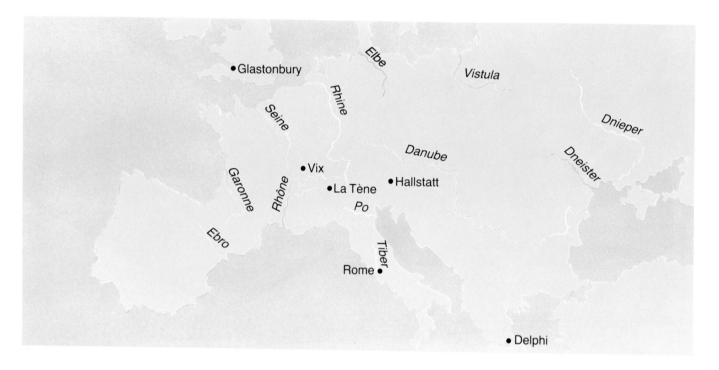

The Iron Age in Europe

Iron age

Iron was known thousands of years ago, even if very uncommon. It only came into general use with the Hittites between 1400 and 1200 B.C. Methods of smelting arrived in Greece about 1000 B.C. and into central Europe two or three centuries later. By about 600 B.C. iron working had started in Britain.

The Celts

If they were not here already, the people known as the Celts certainly came here with the beginning of the iron age. A loosely connected group of peoples, they occupied, at its greatest extent, a wide band of territory stretching across Europe from Ireland to Turkey. They were strong enough to attack Rome in 390 B.C. and Delphi in 278 B.C. but never disciplined enough to form a proper empire. Classical writers said they were quarrelsome and boastful with a childish love of personal finery. They were said to fight from two-horse, two-wheeled chariots and so scornful of death that they fought not only without armour but completely naked. They were brave and light-hearted, loved poetry and learning but were high-spirited and unstable.

Celtic war band

124

Salt mine

Hallstatt

The first site to show evidence of the earliest iron working in Europe was Hallstatt in Austria. In 1848, a large cemetery was discovered. The bodies were dated to about 650 B.C. and the graves were rich in iron swords and other weapons. The wealth of the nearby settlement had been built on huge deposits of salt – a vital substance for everyone. The Hallstatt peoples (probably Celts) spread across Austria, Switzerland, Southern Germany, France, Belgium and Britain. Their settlements in South East Britain are little different from late bronze age sites. We don't really know if the newcomers arrived in small peaceful bands or invaded under their chieftains.

Chariot burials

These are known in Britain but are more common on the continent of Europe. The dead person was laid by a wagon with rich grave goods. A wooden hut was built over the wagon or chariot and earth piled on top of it to make a barrow. The most famous is that of the 'Princess' at Vix, on the upper Seine in France. The body was that of a woman in her thirties and, apart from the normal grave goods such as flagons, plates, harness and chariot metalwork, there was a Greek cup and an enormous bronze cauldron decorated with beautifully sculpted figures. It stands over five feet tall and if filled with liquid, would hold almost 270 gallons. The title 'Princess' was given because of a gold head band or crown which was also found in the grave.

La Tène

This is the name of a place on Lake Neuchâtel in Switzerland, where, in the last century, more than fifty swords, some still in their scabbards, were discovered. They had beautiful patterns of twisting lines worked into their design. This style appeared on many objects from the later iron age, and was exported to Britain where it found expression, for example, on the backs of these metal mirrors.

Bronze objects with La Tène patterns

Lake villages

Occasionally, a tribe would feel safer if protected by water. A moat could be dug round the huts but it was easier to make artificial islands in a lake or swamp. This was done at Glastonbury in Somerset. The lake vil-lagers lived by farming and also by fishing from dug-out canoes. They were good carpenters, potters and metal workers. They turned wooden items on pole lathes and had looms for weaving. Lake villages were also to be found in the margins of continental European lakes.

Names and coins

The Belgae, another people who invaded Britain, came here from about 75 B.C. onward. These were the first Britons to make their own coins – gold ones to start with, then silver and bronze. They are also the first people in our history to whom we can put names. These we know partly from the coins, partly from writers such as Julius Caesar. Thus we can point out the tribal areas of the Cantiaci, Silures, Iceni, Parisi, Trinovantes, Atrebates and Catuvellauni. We even know the names of some of their leaders, for example Tasciovanus and Cunobelinus, Shakespeare's Cymbeline, were kings of the Catuvellauni.

Early Celtic coins

Living places

Apart from hill forts and lake villages, many iron age people probably lived in large, round farmhouses, like the one that was excavated and then rebuilt at Little Woodbury. From posthole marks in the ground, it was possible to work out that the farmstead had consisted of a sizable, circular plan dwelling, several pens and huts for animals and storage plus a very large number of pits in which to keep the grain stores.

Butser Iron Age farm

Hill forts

All over England, but particularly in the south east, iron age peoples built themselves hill forts for protection. The area enclosed by the defences might be as small as half an acre or as large as 200 acres. Some were little more than cattle enclosures, some were temporary hiding places in time of danger, others were lived in permanently. A common pattern was one or more ditches dug all round the top of a hill and the dirt piled up to make an embankment, behind which the defenders could shelter and from where they could bombard the enemy with sling stones.

Maiden Castle, Dorset

Two ways of looking at our past may help you to understand the lengths of time involved. The first shows a 100 metre school sports day race. The old stone age takes well over 99 metres: the middle and new stone ages, the bronze and iron ages, together with the whole of recorded history would take up a smaller measurement than the length of your running shoe!'

The second way might be to compare Man's entire existence on earth to an hour's T.V. programme. You would watch the old stone age for over 59 minutes and only go on to the rest of prehistory and history as the credit titles start to roll!'